Manju Malhi
Classic Indian Recipes

Manju Malhi
Classic Indian Recipes
75 *signature dishes*

hamlyn

An Hachette UK Company
www.hachette.co.uk

First published in Great Britain in 2011 by
Hamlyn, a division of Octopus Publishing Group Ltd
Endeavour House
189 Shaftesbury Avenue
London
WC2H 8JY
www.octopusbooks.co.uk

ISBN 978-0-600-62235-2

A CIP catalogue record for this book is available from the British Library

Printed and bound in China

10 9 8 7 6 5 4 3 2 1

Both metric and imperial measurements are given for the recipes.
Use one set of measures only, not a mixture of both.

Ovens should be preheated to the specified temperature. If using a
fan-assisted oven, follow the manufacturer's instructions for adjusting
the time and temperature. Grills should also be preheated.

This books includes dishes made with nuts and nut derivatives.
It is advisable for those with known allergic reactions to nuts and nut
derivatives and those who may be potentially vulnerable to these
allergies, such as pregnant and nursing mothers, invalids, the elderly,
babies and children, to avoid dishes made with nuts and nut oils.
It is also prudent to check the labels of preprepared ingredients for
the possible inclusion of nut derivatives.

The Department of Health advises that eggs should not be consumed
raw. This book contains some dishes made with raw or lightly cooked
eggs. It is prudent for more vulnerable people such as pregnant and
nursing mothers, invalids, the elderly, babies and young children to
avoid uncooked or lightly cooked dishes made with eggs.

Meat and poultry should be cooked thoroughly. To test if poultry is
cooked, pierce the flesh through the thickest part with a skewer or fork
– the juices should run clear, never pink or red.

Contents

Introduction

Indian hospitality is legendary. Indians believe that they are honoured if they share their mealtimes with guests, and even the poorest people are willing to share their food. This is also a tradition that is now fast becoming the norm in Western society. This book represents my take on good classic Indian food – whether cooked for the family or for guests. I have also tried to ensure that the ingredients for the recipes are as accessible as possible, and to use techniques that are simple to follow and easy to understand. The gadgets required are minimal and the food is prepared using fresh ingredients and designed to match the modern Indian's twenty first-century lifestyle.

In compiling these recipes, I have had to consider that there is no such thing as 'Indian cuisine' but rather there are various cuisines of India, and this is reflected in the dishes I've included from the widely diverse regions of the sub-continent. The scope of Indian cooking is vast and encompasses a wide range of geographic and climatic conditions, centuries of history, and many religions and cultures. However, classic home food is also heavily influenced by the food found in restaurants, cafés and street stalls, so there are plenty of recipes here that have their origins in commercial kitchens.

The art of spicing and the choice of ingredients differ from region to region in India as well as from one cook to the next. Indian food cannot be separated easily from its social and religious context. The two religions that have had the most influence on Indian food are Hinduism and Islam. The Hindu vegetarian tradition is widespread in India, although many Hindus eat meat now. Strict vegetarianism is generally confined to the south of India and the state of Gujarat in the west. Beef from the holy cow is strictly taboo for Hindus and pork is strictly taboo for the Muslims.

India also has an extraordinary ability to absorb and make use of foreign gastronomic influences. Among the most notable are the Arabian, Iranian, Mogul and Chinese. Of these, the Moguls, who invaded India, arguably made the deepest impact. They brought with them exotic spices, dried fruit and nuts. The Indians combined these with milk and cream to make rich Mughlai dishes, including creamy kormas and fragrant biryanis and pulaos (spiced rice dishes).

INTRODUCTION

Spices

Indian cooking combines six basic tastes: sweet, sour, salty, spicy or pungent, bitter and astringent, and a well-balanced meal will contain all six elements. Spices contribute to many of the flavours, and the most important spices include chillies, mustard seeds, cumin, turmeric, fenugreek, ginger, coriander and asafoetida. Although salt is not considered a spice, it is often used to assist in bringing out the flavours of spices in Indian food. In sweet dishes, cardamom, cinnamon, nutmeg and saffron are popular.

Store cupboard essentials I tend to have in my storecupboard five 'all-round' spices – cumin, coriander, garam masala, turmeric and chilli powder. To me these are the essential spices in most savoury Indian dishes. Storing them away from sunlight, moisture and heat gives them a longer shelf-life. Whole spices, if stored properly, should last for at least 6 months, while ground spices will keep their flavour for only around 3–6 months. I don't tend to buy spices in bulk and prefer to shop for them regularly to ensure freshness and flavour. If you can't find your ingredients locally, there are several spice markets, especially online, which ship spices – as well as other ingredients – anywhere in the world. Each spice has a distinctive role in Indian cooking, which means it will also have a distinctive flavour. So, for example, never substitute saffron for turmeric, as turmeric imparts a bitter taste, while saffron (which is also the most expensive spice in the world) possesses a 'sea air' aroma with a warm, sweet taste.

Grinding your spices It's worth investing in a small pestle and mortar to grind most of your major whole spices. The mortar is the bowl and the pestle is the rounded stick implement. If you're planning to use your coffee mill instead, then make sure that you clean it out once you have ground your spices, otherwise your coffee will taste of them. A good way of cleaning a coffee mill is by grinding some uncooked rice grains and then wiping the inside of the grinding container with kitchen paper.

8

Using chillies Various chillies are used in Indian cuisine and a general rule-of-thumb is that the smaller the chilli, the hotter it will be, so your dishes will be hotter as a result. However, when chillies are heated they do lose their pungency slightly.

Key ingredients

Apart from spices, the main flavouring ingredients are milk and its products, such as yogurt and cream. Onions and garlic are used in many savoury dishes, but certain Hindu sects prohibit their use. Coconut oil, ghee (clarified butter), sesame oil and mustard oil are the most common cooking oils in Indian cuisine, although olive oil is used in the Portuguese-influenced region of Goa. However, with the fast-paced lifestyles dominating the cities, it is now acceptable to use sunflower, vegetable or rapeseed oil in Indian cooking.

Pulses These are common across India, with the most widely used ones being chickpeas, black lentils, gram lentils, red lentils, yellow lentils or pigeon peas, kidney beans, black-eyed beans and mung beans. In the north, pulse dishes – or dals – are quite thick, while in the south, they have a more soup-like consistency. Some pulses require overnight soaking before cooking, while others can be prepared in minutes.

Breads Indian breads are varied. The simplest bread is the chapati or roti, which is made from a dough of water and wheat flour, and then heated on a griddle or tawa. Baste the chapati with ghee or butter and it becomes a paratha. If deep-fried, it is called a poori in the north and a luchi in the east. Another deep-fried bread with a stuffing is the kachori. Baked in an oven it becomes a naan.

Rice The best Indian rice is the famous basmati. Basmati means 'the fragrant one' and it is predominantly grown in the Dehra Dun Valley, in the foothills of the Himalayas. Served on special occasions, it has long grains, is yellowish in colour and has a slightly earthy aroma.

Drink Traditionally, nothing is drunk with an Indian meal other than water. If you're aiming to serve a wine with your meal, be aware that the spices in the dishes may well affect the flavours in the wine. There are, however, many beverages and alcoholic drinks on the market specifically created to match Indian food and its spices, which should help you make the right choice of tipple.

Cooking techniques

Techniques used in Indian cooking include braising, for dishes such as korma, and slow oven baking (dumpukht). By contrast, the tandoor and its resulting tandoori cuisine, has achieved popularity the world over. The tandoor introduces an earthy flavour to food. The meat is marinated with spices and yogurt. The clay oven is traditionally a pot that is sunk neck-deep in the ground. Charcoal is put inside it and heated, and it is the heat generated by the hot charcoal that does the cooking. The tandoori is hotter than conventional ovens, so the food is crisp on the outside and moist and tender on the inside, as with tandoori naan breads and tikkas.

In the West, the word 'curry' has become synonymous with Indian food. So going for a curry in the Western hemisphere would mean going for an Indian meal. However, in Indian culinary terms, a curry means simply gravy or a dish containing gravy. Stainless steel and non-stick pans are suitable for cooking Indian food, especially when frying onions or preparing gravies for curry dishes.

As with the cooking of any kind of dish, it's good to have all your ingredients in front of you and to cut and prepare everything before you actually start to cook. Sharp knives also make life easier in the kitchen. With a good knife you can do most of the tasks necessary with the greatest of ease. Wooden spoons of all shapes and sizes will be handy, as will measuring spoons for the measuring of ingredients – particularly ground spices. Once you've become familiar and more comfortable with the repertoire of spices in Indian cooking, feel free to add, remove or reduce spices when preparing dishes in order to make it your own.

Basic skills

These are some of my key tips for preparing any Indian cuisine:

- Always preheat your pan before adding any oil.
- When assembling spices for cooking, keep the whole spices separate from the ground spices.
- It is important to temper spices: this is the process of dry-roasting or toasting the spices by warming them up in a hot dry pan and, as soon as the aromas are released, allowing them to cool and then grinding them to a powder to make spice mixtures.
- Often, whole spices are fried in oil, which intensifies their flavours. This technique is also sometimes used to garnish or 'finish off' a dish.

- When heating spices, make sure they do not burn or your dishes will taste burnt. This also applies to onions, so remove any burnt onions if possible or start again with a clean pan.
- If you find that your curry is too spicy hot, you can add cream, coconut milk, sugar or tomatoes to moderate the heat. (Cream and coconut should only be added if the recipe already contains those ingredients.) Do bear in mind, however, that it is always easier to increase the chilli heat of a dish than to reduce it.
- Adding a piece of raw potato in a dish during cooking will reduce the saltiness. (The potato is removed before serving and the dish can be topped up with water if necessary.)
- Rice should only be reheated once, and served piping hot.

It would be fair to say that every day I learn something new about Indian food, as it is a cuisine that is changing continuously, due to innovative cooks. This is not only true just in India but abroad as well. Something that remains constant, though, is the range of spices used to flavour Indian food – as well as the enjoyment of cooking, which I hope you will also find when trying these recipes.

Meat & Poultry

Rich Lamb Curry
Mutton Nihari

SERVES 2−3

5 tablespoons sunflower or vegetable oil

1 onion, finely chopped

4–6 green cardamoms

2–3 black cardamoms

500 g (1 lb) lamb steaks, chopped into 2.5 cm (1 inch) cubes

½ teaspoon turmeric

½ teaspoon salt

½ teaspoon ground cumin

¼ teaspoon chilli powder

½ teaspoon ground coriander

4 garlic cloves, crushed

generous pinch of garam masala (see below)

pinch of freshly grated nutmeg

1 teaspoon peeled and grated fresh root ginger

FOR THE
GARAM MASALA
(SPICE MIX)

1 teaspoon whole cloves

3–4 bay leaves

2 green cardamom pods, seeds only

4 black cardamom pods, seeds only

1 teaspoon caraway seeds (optional)

12 black peppercorns

½ teaspoon freshly grated nutmeg

Mutton Nihari is a dish from Lucknow in northern India eaten mainly amongst Muslim communities at breakfast. It originally hails from Pakistan and though widely known to be prepared with beef shank, many variations use lamb or mutton.

1 To make the garam masala spice mix: Heat a pan and add all the ingredients except the nutmeg. Stir for 30 seconds to release the aromas. Remove from the heat, add the nutmeg, then grind the mixture to a fine powder in a coffee mill or using a pestle and mortar. Store any leftover mix in an airtight container away from sunlight for up to 6 months.

2 Heat 3 tablespoons of the oil in a saucepan and fry the onion for 12–15 minutes until golden brown. Remove from the pan and set aside.

3 Using the same pan, add the remaining 2 tablespoons of oil and put back on the heat. When the oil is hot, add the whole green and black cardamoms. When they sizzle, add the lamb and fry, stirring occasionally, for 8–10 minutes until browned all over.

4 Add the turmeric and salt with 400 ml (14 fl oz) of just-boiled water. Let the meat simmer for 20 minutes or until it is tender. Add the cumin, chilli powder, coriander and garlic, and mix well. Return the fried onions to the pan and cook for another 10 minutes until the sauce begins to thicken.

5 Sprinkle over the garam masala and pinch of grated nutmeg, then top with the fresh ginger. Serve hot.

Chettinad Chicken
Kozhi Chettinad

SERVES 2−3

2 tablespoons vegetable oil

¼ teaspoon brown or black mustard seeds

pinch of asafoetida

5–6 curry leaves, roughly chopped

400 g (13 oz) chicken fillets, skinned and cut into 2.5 cm (1 inch) cubes

1 teaspoon ground cumin

½ teaspoon ground coriander

¼ teaspoon turmeric

¼ teaspoon salt

¼ teaspoon hot chilli powder

2 tablespoons coconut cream

juice of ½ lime

1 teaspoon peeled and finely grated fresh root ginger

30 g (1 oz) coriander leaves, roughly chopped

Chettinad is a region in India where most of the curries are hot but deliciously flavoured with whole and ground spices. I've reduced the amount of chilli in this recipe – it's customary to use 1 teaspoon of hot chilli powder per person.

1 Heat the oil in a heavy-based pan or wok over a medium heat. To check that it has reached the right temperature, sprinkle in a few of the mustard seeds: if they pop, it is hot enough to add the remainder. Then add the asafoetida and curry leaves and fry for 30 seconds, stirring continuously, until everything is well combined and aromatic. Tip in the chicken and fry for 5 minutes over a medium heat or until golden brown. Add the cumin, coriander, turmeric, salt and chilli powder, and cook for 2 minutes, stirring continuously.

2 In a bowl, mix 4 tablespoons of boiling water with the coconut cream and add to the chicken. Stir for a minute, then add the lime juice. Mix thoroughly, simmer for 3–4 minutes, then add the ginger and simmer for another minute or until the chicken is cooked through. Garnish with coriander leaves and serve hot with Basmati Chawal (see page 124) and Avial (see page 84).

Cardamom-flavoured Lamb Patties
Galouti Kabab

**MAKES 4
PATTIES**

1 tablespoon Bengal gram or channa dal or yellow split peas

250 g (8 oz) minced lamb, minced several times until smooth

1 teaspoon peeled and roughly grated fresh root ginger

2 garlic cloves, crushed

¼ teaspoon mango powder (amchur)

15 g (½ oz) butter

1 teaspoon hot chilli powder

2 green cardamoms, seeds only, crushed

½ teaspoon salt

2 teaspoons vegetable oil

1 medium red or white onion, thinly sliced, to serve

There are hundreds of varieties of kababs such as Kakori Kababs, Galawat Ke Kababs, Shami Kababs and Seekh Kababs. Galouti means 'melt in the mouth' where the meat has been diced, minced and pounded to a fine paste and then flavoured with herbs and spices.

1 Pick over the channa dal to check for small stones. Place a small pan over a low heat and roast the channa dal for 2 minutes, making sure that it doesn't burn. Grind it into a fine powder using a coffee mill. Mix together with all the remaining ingredients except the vegetable oil and onion, cover and refrigerate for 2 hours or overnight. Wet your hands and divide the mince into 4 equal parts. Shape each into a flat, round pattie about 1.5 cm (¾ inch) thick.

2 Heat the oil in a frying pan and shallow-fry the patties over a medium heat, cooking boths side for about 10 minutes or until cooked through, making sure each side browns evenly. Alternatively, preheat a grill to medium and grill for 10 minutes on each side, or until cooked through. Serve hot with Phulka (see page 106) and onion rings.

Creamy Chicken Tikka
Malai Murgh Tikka

SERVES 2

1 teaspoon lemon juice

¼ teaspoon salt

2 boneless and skinless chicken breasts, about 300 g (10 oz), cut into 2.5 cm (1 inch) pieces

2 tablespoons Greek-style natural unsweetened yogurt

30 g (1 oz) butter

1 tablespoon double cream

1 tablespoon adrak lahsun ka masala (see below)

3 green cardamom pods, seeds only

½ teaspoon ground cumin

½ teaspoon freshly grated nutmeg

2 green finger chillies, finely chopped

1 tablespoon groundnut or vegetable oil

2 tablespoons Cheddar cheese, finely grated

FOR THE ADRAK LAHSUN KA MASALA (GINGER AND GARLIC PASTE) MAKES 100 ML (3½ FL OZ)

125 g (4 oz) fresh root ginger, peeled and coarsely chopped

125 g (4 oz) garlic cloves

It may seem unconventional or somewhat inauthentic to use Cheddar cheese as an ingredient, but Cheddar adds extra creaminess to this dish from Lucknow.

1 To make the adrak lahsun ka masala: in a food processor, blend the ginger and garlic together to a smooth paste. If necessary, add 15 ml (1 tablespoon) cold water. Store in a covered container in the refrigerator for up to 2 weeks.

2 Sprinkle the lemon juice and salt over the chicken pieces, cover and set aside.

3 Mix the yogurt, half the butter, the cream, adrak lahsun ka masala, cardamom seeds, cumin, nutmeg, chillies, oil and cheese, and blend into a smooth paste. Pour over the chicken, making sure it is all well coated, and marinate the meat for 1 hour, covered, in the refrigerator.

4 Soak 4–6 wooden skewers in cold water for 15 minutes to prevent them burning. Skewer the chicken and barbecue or grill under a preheated grill, for 10 minutes on each side until light brown and cooked through, or simply bake in a preheated oven, 180°C/350°F/gas mark 4, for 15 minutes or until the chicken is cooked. Halfway through cooking, baste with the remaining butter, melted.

5 Serve the skewers hot or cold with Jeera Chawal (see page 120).

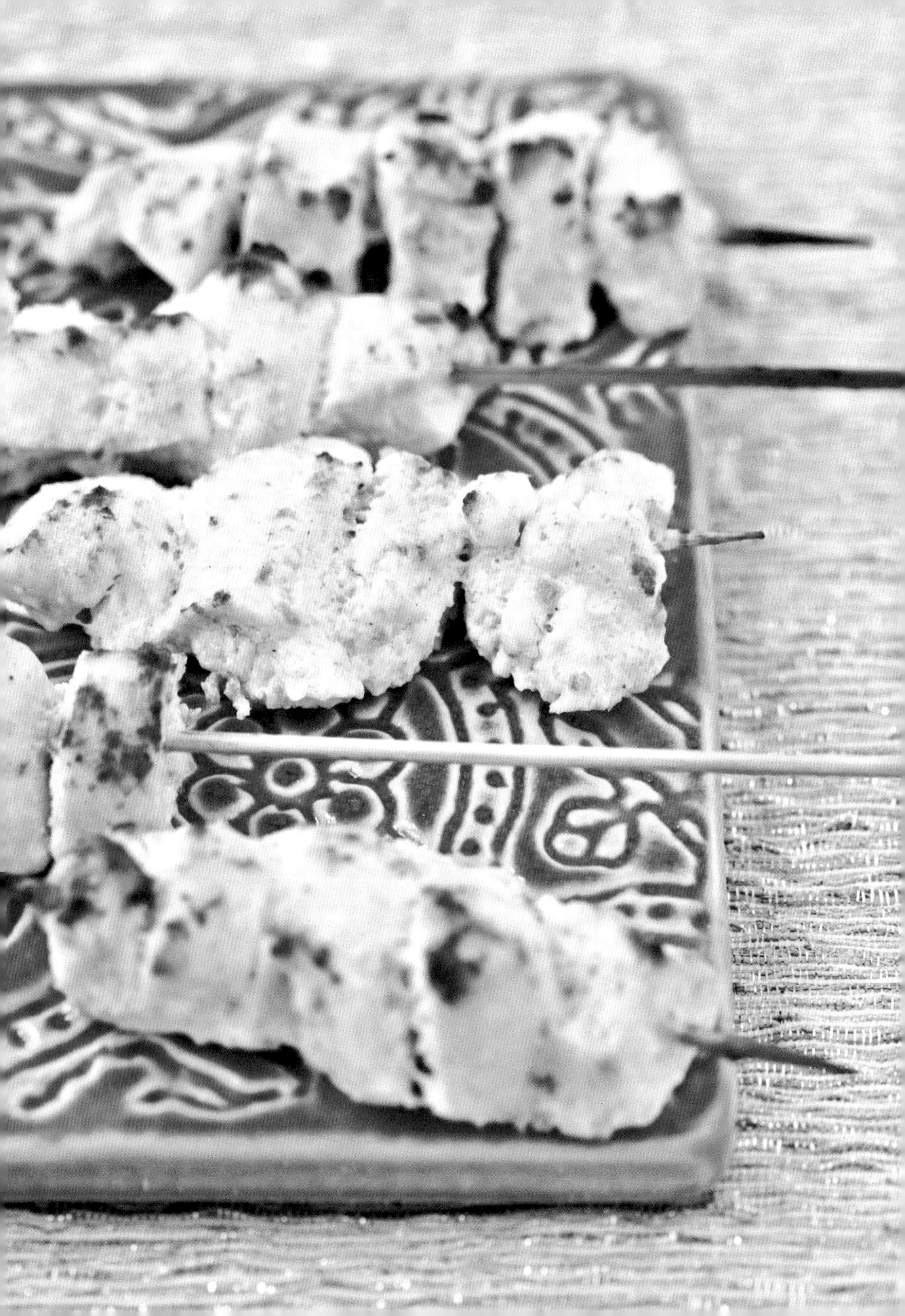

Meat Curry
Mangshor Jhol

SERVES 2–3

300 g (10 oz) stewing lamb, cut into 3.5–4 cm (1½–1¾ inch) cubes

3 tablespoons natural unsweetened yogurt

2 tablespoons mustard oil or vegetable oil

1 bay leaf (optional)

1 x 2.5 cm (1 inch) cinnamon stick

2 cloves

2 green cardamoms, bruised

1 medium onion, thinly sliced

2 garlic cloves, crushed

1 teaspoon peeled and finely grated fresh root ginger

½ teaspoon turmeric

½ teaspoon hot chilli powder

1 teaspoon ground cumin

½ teaspoon salt

2 green finger chillies, slit lengthways

¼ teaspoon garam masala (see page 14)

Jhol is a curry from eastern India where the sauce is not too thick. This dish can be served with plain basmati rice and fried vegetables.

1 Marinate the meat in the yogurt for 20 minutes, covered, in the refrigerator.

2 Heat the oil in a heavy-based pan. Add the bay leaf (if using) the cinnamon, cloves and cardamoms, and sauté for 30 seconds. Add the onion and garlic. Stir-fry over a medium heat for 3 minutes, then add the ginger, followed by the turmeric, chilli powder, cumin and salt, and mix well. Add the marinated meat and green chillies. Stir and cook on a low heat for 15 minutes.

3 Add 400 ml (14 fl oz) boiling water, cover and cook on a low heat for 30 minutes until the meat is cooked through. Sprinkle over the garam masala.

4 Serve hot with Basmati Chawal (see page 124).

Lamb Kebabs
Kakori Kabab

MAKES 8−10
KABABS

4 tablespoons channa
  dal or Bengal gram or
  yellow split peas

4 green cardamoms,
  seeds only

1 black cardamom,
  seeds only

10 black peppercorns

2 cloves (optional)

3 dried large red chillies

3 tablespoons vegetable
  oil

1 small onion, finely
  chopped

500 g (1 lb) minced lamb

1 teaspoon salt

¼ teaspoon freshly
  grated nutmeg

1 medium egg, beaten

*These kababs are softer versions of Seekh Kababs made with finely
ground mince and often a combination of more than 50 spices.
This recipe from northern India uses six spices but they are full
of flavour nonetheless.*

1 Soak 8−10 wooden skewers in cold water for 15 minutes.
Check the channa dal for small stones.

2 Heat a small pan over a medium heat and add the
channa dal, cardamom seeds, peppercorns, cloves (if using)
and red chillies. Stir for 30 seconds to release the aromas.
Remove from the heat and allow to cool. Grind everything
to a fine powder in a coffee mill or use a pestle and mortar.

3 In a frying pan, heat 2 tablespoons of the oil and fry the
onion over a medium heat for 5 minutes until light golden.

4 Grind the minced lamb into a smooth paste in a food
processor with the remaining oil. Add the fried onion,
ground spices, salt, nutmeg and egg. Mix well. Using
wet hands, take a golf-ball-sized lump of the mixture
and press it tightly around a skewer in a sausage
shape. Repeat with the remaining mince.

5 Place under a preheated grill, or on a
barbecue, and cook for 10−15 minutes on each
side or until cooked through. Serve hot with
Pudinay ki Chatni (see page 128).

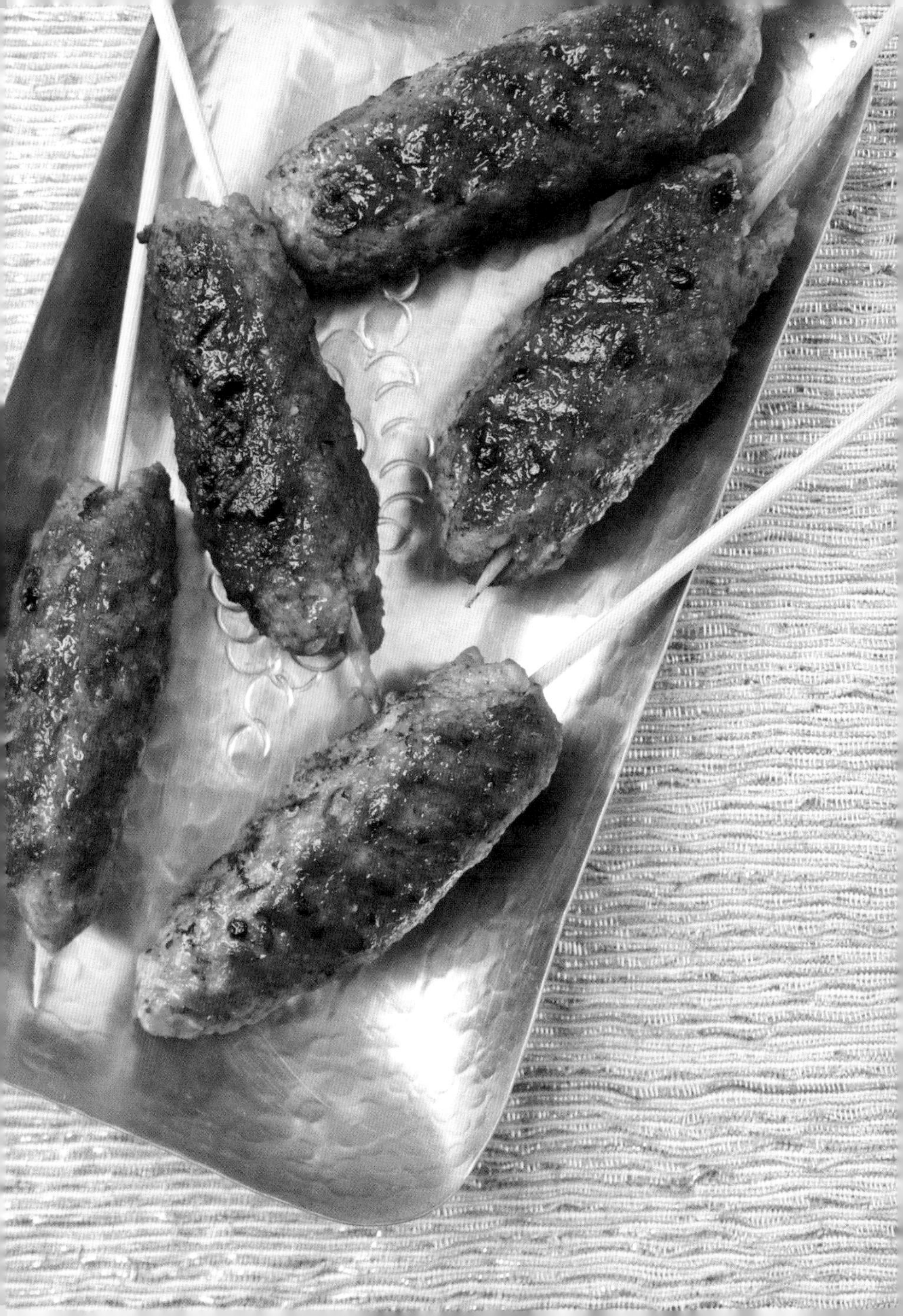

Kerala Chicken Stew
Kerala Kozhi Eshstu

SERVES 4

4 green finger chillies, roughly chopped, plus 2 more, slit lengthways, to garnish

¼ teaspoon turmeric

¼ teaspoon ground coriander

¼ teaspoon ground cinnamon

1 teaspoon peeled and finely grated fresh root ginger

4 garlic cloves, roughly chopped

¼ teaspoon salt

4 tablespoons groundnut oil

5–6 curry leaves

2–4 cloves

1 large onion, thinly sliced

1 kg (2 lb) chicken drumsticks and thighs, skinned and pricked

200 ml (7 fl oz) coconut milk

Keralan cuisine has adopted colonial British stew recipes, adding spices to make them their own. In southern India, stew is made with coconut milk and Malabar Coast spices.

1 In a blender or with a pestle and mortar, blitz the chillies, turmeric, coriander, cinnamon, ginger, garlic and salt with 1 tablespoon of the oil and 2 tablespoons of cold water to make a coarse paste.

2 Heat the remaining oil in a heavy-based pan. Add the curry leaves, cloves and onion, and fry over a medium heat for 3 minutes. Add the paste and fry for a minute. Tip in the chicken pieces and fry for 10 minutes on a medium to low heat.

3 Rinse out the blender or mortar that contained the paste with 200 ml (7 fl oz) cold water. Mix this with the coconut milk. Pour over the chicken and mix well. Cover the pan and simmer for 15 minutes, or until the chicken is cooked.

4 Garnish with the slit green chillies and serve hot with Elemicha Sadam (see page 122).

Marinated Roast Leg of Lamb
Raan

SERVES 4
1.5 kg (3 lb) leg of lamb, on the bone

3 tablespoons vegetable oil

3 garlic cloves, crushed

250 ml (8 fl oz) natural unsweetened yogurt

1 tablespoon garam masala (see page 14)

1 teaspoon peeled and finely grated fresh root ginger

½ teaspoon salt

¼ teaspoon medium-hot chilli powder

5–6 saffron strands

Fit for an emperor, Raan is a leg of lamb that has been marinated in a yogurt and spice mixture, then it is traditionally roasted on a spit over a wood fire.

1 Prick the flesh of the lamb all over with a skewer. Mix all the remaining ingredients together to make the marinade and smear it thickly over the lamb. Place on a plate and cover, then leave to marinate in the refrigerator for a couple of hours.

2 Preheat the oven to 180°C/350°F/gas mark 4. Put the lamb in a roasting tin and cover with foil, ensuring that it doesn't touch the lamb. Cook for 2 hours until the meat is tender. Halfway through cooking, baste the lamb with any juices in the pan. At the end of the 2 hours, remove the foil and cook the lamb for 30–40 minutes more until the lamb achieves a golden colour. Take the meat out of the oven, cover loosely with foil and leave to rest in a warm place for about 15 minutes.

3 Make a gravy with the remaining juices from the roasting tin by stirring in 5–7 tablespoons boiling water and simmering over a medium heat for 3 minutes. Carve the lamb and pour the spicy gravy over the meat. Serve with Aloo Gobhi (see page 72) and Pudinay ki Chatni (see page 128).

Chilli Chicken
Mirch Waala Murgh

SERVES 2

- 1 tablespoon dark soy sauce
- ½ teaspoon hot chilli powder
- ¼ teaspoon salt
- 1 tablespoon cornflour
- 1 teaspoon peeled and finely grated fresh root ginger
- 2 garlic cloves, finely chopped
- 1 tablespoon malt vinegar
- 1 tablespoon tomato purée
- 1 teaspoon demerara sugar
- 2 tablespoons vegetable oil or groundnut oil
- 1 medium onion, finely chopped
- 2 boneless and skinless chicken breasts, about 300 g (10 oz), cut into 2.5 cm (1 inch) cubes
- 2 green finger chillies, slit lengthways
- ¼ teaspoon ground white pepper
- 4 spring onions, sliced

East Indians have added a few Chinese touches to this traditional dish to create Chilli Chicken. Chinese-influenced dishes appeared to originate in the Shantung communities from north-east China: blacksmiths and tailors brought their particular kind of Chinese cuisine into India.

1 At least 45 minutes ahead, mix together the soy sauce, chilli powder, salt, cornflour, ginger, garlic, vinegar, tomato purée and sugar.

2 Heat 1 tablespoon of the oil in a heavy-based pan. Fry the onion over a medium heat for 5 minutes until soft and translucent. Remove from the heat and mix the fried onions with the soy sauce paste. Add the chicken and stir to coat. Cover and leave to marinate for 30 minutes in the refrigerator.

3 Heat the pan again with the remaining oil. Add the green chillies and white pepper and fry over a low heat for a minute. Then add the marinated chicken pieces with the marinade, most of which will have been soaked up by the chicken, and fry for 10 minutes until the chicken is cooked.

4 Garnish with spring onions and serve hot.

Hot Lamb Curry
Laal Maas

SERVES 2 – 3

500 g (1 lb) stewing lamb, cut into 2.5 cm (1 inch) cubes

2 teaspoons hot chilli powder

2 garlic cloves, crushed

¼ teaspoon turmeric

½ teaspoon ground coriander

½ large onion, finely chopped

4 tablespoons natural unsweetened yogurt

¼ teaspoon salt

2 tablespoons groundnut oil

1 small onion, thickly sliced

30 g (1 oz) coriander leaves, roughly chopped

Laal Maas from Rajasthan is lamb cooked in garlic, coriander and enough red chilli to make your hair stand on end. I've used chilli powder instead of the traditional 12–15 dried red chillies. The chilli heat of this curry is reflected in its name: Laal means red.

1 Mix together the lamb, chilli, garlic, turmeric, coriander, chopped onion, yogurt and salt. Cover and leave to marinate for about 30 minutes in the refrigerator.

2 Heat the oil in a heavy-based pan, add the sliced onion and fry for 4–5 minutes until translucent. Add the lamb mix and cook gently for 8 minutes to brown the meat.

3 Add 300 ml (½ pint) boiling water, cover and simmer over a low heat, stirring occasionally, for 30 minutes or until the meat is tender.

4 Garnish with coriander leaves and serve hot with Basmati Chawal (see page 124).

Whole Tandoori Chicken
Murgh Tandoori

SERVES 2−3

1 x 1.5 kg (3 lb) chicken

4 tablespoons natural unsweetened yogurt

1 teaspoon garam masala (see page 14)

4 tablespoons single cream

2 tablespoons medium-hot paprika

1 teaspoon medium-hot chilli powder

1 teaspoon ground cumin

2 tablespoons lemon juice

2 tablespoons vegetable oil

1 teaspoon salt

½ teaspoon turmeric

1 tablespoon tomato purée

4 garlic cloves, crushed

2 teaspoons peeled and finely grated fresh root ginger

The traditional way of making Tandoori Chicken is by cooking it in a tandoor. These days, you will rarely find tandoors in Indian homes but roasting in an oven does provide a similar effect.

1 Well ahead or the night before, prick the chicken all over and make a few slits about 2.5 cm (1 inch) long in the skin. Mix all the remaining ingredients into a smooth paste and smother the marinade generously all over the chicken skin. Cover and refrigerate for 8 hours or overnight.

2 Preheat the oven to 180°C/350°F/gas mark 4. Place the chicken in a roasting tin and cover it with foil. Roast in the centre of the oven for 1 hour 30 minutes. Halfway through cooking, baste with a little of the marinade. Remove from the oven and leave the chicken in a warm place to rest for 20 minutes. Carve and serve either hot or cold with Dhaniyein ki Chatni (see page 126).

Spiced Chicken Kebabs
Murgh Seekh Kabab

**MAKES 10
KABABS**

- 1 **medium egg**
- 1 **teaspoon ground
  cumin**
- ½ **teaspoon ground
  white pepper**
- ¼ **teaspoon salt**
- 1 **teaspoon hot chilli
  powder**
- 1 **tablespoon vegetable
  oil**
- 6–8 **cashew nuts,
  ground (optional)**
- ½ **small onion, finely
  chopped**
- 2 **teaspoons peeled and
  finely grated fresh
  root ginger**
- 30 g (1 oz) **coriander
  leaves, chopped**
- ½ **teaspoon garam
  masala (see page 14)**
- 500 g (1 lb) **chicken
  meat, minced**
- **vegetable oil, for
  basting**
- 1 **lemon, sliced
  lengthways into 6,
  to serve**
- 2 **medium red onions,
  thinly sliced into
  rings, to serve**

*The Moguls revolutionized the art of Indian cooking with their
kababs and tikkas: small pieces of meat and vegetables usually
cooked on skewers in a tandoor. These kababs can be served as
snacks, starters or even as the main course itself. This recipe
is great for barbecues.*

1 Preheat the oven to 180°C/350°C/gas mark 4 or turn
the grill on to medium. Soak 10 wooden skewers in cold
water for 15 minutes to prevent them burning.

2 In a small bowl, whisk together the egg, cumin, pepper,
salt, chilli powder and vegetable oil. Fold in the cashew
nuts (if using), the onion, ginger, coriander leaves and
garam masala. Add this mixture to the chicken and mix
everything together.

3 Have a bowl of cold water ready for dipping your hands
into. With wet hands, pick up a portion of the chicken
mixture slightly larger than a golf ball and wrap it tightly
around each skewer to make a thin sausage shape.

4 Place the skewers directly on the oven shelves or under
the grill for 10 minutes on each side, turning and basting
them with oil at least twice.

5 Serve hot or cold with lemon slices and onion rings.

Lamb Rice
Hyderabadi Biryani

SERVES 4

500 g (1 lb) stewing
lamb, cut into bite-
sized chunks

2 teaspoons adrak
lahsun ka masala
(see page 20)

2.5 cm (1 inch)
cinnamon stick

2 cloves

4 green cardamoms,
seeds only

½–1 teaspoon medium-
hot chilli powder

1 tablespoon natural
unsweetened yogurt

1 tablespoon lemon
juice

6 tablespoons
groundnut oil

½ teaspoon salt

1 medium onion, thinly
sliced

200 g (7 oz) white
basmati rice, or any
other long-grain rice

4 tablespoons full-fat or
semi-skimmed milk

a few saffron strands

15 g (½ oz) butter or
ghee

*The cuisine of Hyderabad, the capital city of Andhra Pradesh,
ranges from the Hyderabadi style with its strong Islamic influence,
to a pure Andhra hot and spicy style. Hyderabad is also famous
for its biryanis – rice dishes flavoured with meat or vegetables.*

1 Mix the lamb with the adrak lahsun ka masala,
cinnamon, cloves, cardamoms, chilli, yogurt, lemon juice,
1 tablespoon of the oil and the salt. Cover and refrigerate
for 30–45 minutes.

2 Heat 3 tablespoons of the oil in a small frying pan
and fry the onion for 5 minutes, or until crisp and golden
brown. Set aside.

3 Rinse the rice thoroughly in cold running water and
place in a pan with 400 ml (14 fl oz) boiling water.
Cover and boil for 8 minutes or until the rice is half-
cooked: the grains should be soft on the outside but still
hard in the centre.

4 Gently warm the milk and soak the saffron strands in it
for a few minutes.

5 Preheat the oven to 180°C/350°F/gas mark 4. Heat the
remaining oil in a heavy-based pan and fry the marinated
meat for 15 minutes until well browned. Stir in the fried
onion. Grease the base of a large heavy-based casserole
with the butter or ghee. Add the meat mixture followed by
the parboiled rice. Pack the rice firmly into the casserole.
Pour the saffron-laced milk over the rice. Cover tightly and
bake in the oven for 45–50 minutes.

6 Serve hot with raitas and Pudinay ki Chatni (see page 128).
It is good with extra fried onions, sultanas and roasted
cashew nuts, too.

Meat Fritters
Mangsher Chop

MAKES 8−10
FRITTERS

3 tablespoons vegetable oil or groundnut oil

1 onion, finely chopped

2 green finger chillies, finely chopped

1 teaspoon peeled and grated fresh root ginger

2 garlic cloves, crushed

½ teaspoon each of salt, turmeric, ground cumin and ground coriander

1 teaspoon tomato purée

500 g (1 lb) minced lamb

2 teaspoons fresh mint leaves, finely chopped

¼ teaspoon garam masala (see page 14)

500 g (1 lb) white or red potatoes, boiled and mashed

½ teaspoon ground white pepper

4 tablespoons dried white breadcrumbs

2 medium eggs, beaten

vegetable oil, for shallow-frying

Most Indians have an image of Bengalis as lovers of fish and sweets. However, snacking is also taken very seriously. Jhol khabar is an afternoon meal consisting of light food, such as shingaras (Bengali samosas) or mangsher chop, a potato patty stuffed with spiced minced lamb, coated with breadcrumbs and shallow-fried.

1 Heat the oil in a heavy-based pan over a medium heat and fry the onion for 5 minutes. Add the chillies, ginger and garlic, and fry for a further 2 minutes. Add ¼ teaspoon salt, the turmeric, cumin and coriander, and mix well.

2 Add the tomato purée, stir in the mince and fry over a medium heat for 3 minutes to brown the meat. Add the mint and fry, stirring often, for 15 minutes or until the mince is cooked. Sprinkle over the garam masala.

3 Mix the mashed potatoes with ¼ teaspoon salt and the white pepper.

4 Spread the breadcrumbs on a flat plate. Take a handful of the mash with wet hands and make a bowl shape. Place 1 tablespoon of the mince in the centre of the mash and pull the edges over it to seal. Shape into a flat, round fritters 7.5 cm (3 inches) in diameter and 1.5 cm (¾ inch) thick. Repeat with the remaining mash and mince.

5 Dip each fritter first in the egg, then coat evenly in breadcrumbs and set aside ready to cook.

6 Heat the oil for shallow-frying in a large frying pan. Fry the fritters in batches on each side for 2 minutes until light golden. Remove and drain on kitchen paper before serving.

Chicken in an Aromatic Coconut Sauce
Galinha Xacuti

SERVES 2–3

4 black peppercorns

4 cloves

1 star anise

1 teaspoon fennel seeds (optional)

3 dried red chillies, stalks removed

3 green cardamoms

½ teaspoon poppy seeds

2 x 2.5 cm (1 inch) cinnamon sticks

¼ teaspoon salt

¼ teaspoon turmeric

½ teaspoon ground cumin

¼ teaspoon ground coriander

2 tablespoons groundnut oil

1 medium white onion, finely chopped

1 garlic clove, finely chopped

400 g (13 oz) boneless chicken thighs and drumsticks

200 ml (7 fl oz) coconut milk

¼ teaspoon tamarind concentrate or paste

grated fresh coconut, to serve

Xacuti, pronounced Shaguti, is a curry from Goa made with coconut, red chillies, tamarind and an aromatic blend of spices. It is traditionally prepared with chicken on the bone and has a hot sweetness to the sauce, which is attributed to the fennel seeds and the coconut.

1 Heat a frying pan and add the peppercorns, cloves, star anise, fennel seeds (if using), red chillies, cardamoms, poppy seeds and cinnamon, and roast for 1 minute. Put the roasted spices in a coffee mill with the salt, turmeric, cumin and coriander, and grind to a coarse powder; alternatively, use a pestle and mortar but do not add the ground spices to the mortar.

2 Heat the oil in the pan and gently fry the onion and garlic for 3 minutes. Add the chicken pieces and sauté for 6–7 minutes, browning them all over. Add the ground spice mixture and stir-fry for a minute, then add 100 ml (3½ fl oz) boiling water and simmer for 5 minutes.

3 Mix the coconut milk with 200 ml (7 fl oz) boiling water, then add to the chicken and simmer for another 6 minutes.

4 Stir in the tamarind and cook for another 5–7 minutes, until it reaches the consistency of runny gravy and the chicken is cooked through. Sprinkle with grated fresh coconut and serve.

Chicken Shahjahani
Shahjahani Murgh

SERVES 2−3

2 tablespoons ghee or butter

2−3 bay leaves

3 black cardamoms

4 green cardamoms

1 piece of cinnamon or cassia bark

4 cloves

8−10 black peppercorns

¼ teaspoon cumin seeds

1 onion, very finely chopped

3 garlic cloves, crushed

1 teaspoon peeled and grated fresh root ginger, plus a few more julienne strips to serve

400 g (13 oz) boneless and skinless chicken breasts, chopped into 3 cm (1¼ inch) pieces

4 tablespoons single cream

8−10 saffron strands

2 tablespoons ground almonds

¼ teaspoon salt

¼ teaspoon ground white pepper

As the name suggests, this dish was created for Shah Jahan. An emperor of the Mogul empire in India during the sixteenth century, he is more notably known for building the Taj Mahal in Agra for his wife Mumtaz.

1 Heat a saucepan or wok and add the ghee or butter. Add the bay leaves, cardamoms, cinnamon or cassia bark, cloves, black peppercorns and cumin seeds to the pan and mix. Then add the onion, garlic and grated ginger, and fry for 3 minutes until lightly browned.

2 Tip in the chicken and fry for 10 minutes until white on the outside. The mixture will look yellowy-white in colour.

3 Place the cream in a bowl and add the saffron. Set aside.

4 Add the ground almonds to the chicken and cook for 2 minutes. Mix in the salt and white pepper, followed by the cream and saffron. Mix well, pour 100 ml (3½ fl oz) water into the pan and cook for a further 2 minutes.

5 Garnish with the julienne strips of ginger and serve hot.

Chicken and Egg Wrap
Kathi Roll

MAKES 6 WRAPS

FOR THE FILLING

2 boneless and skinless chicken breasts, cut into 2.5 cm (1 inch) cubes

1 garlic clove, crushed

1 teaspoon peeled and grated root ginger

1 teaspoon ground cumin

¼ teaspoon turmeric

pinch of garam masala (see page 14)

2 green finger chillies, finely chopped

1 teaspoon tomato purée

1 teaspoon lemon juice

¼ teaspoon salt

1 tablespoon vegetable oil

FOR THE PARATHAS

200 g (7 oz) plain white flour, plus more for dusting

¼ teaspoon salt

1 teaspoon vegetable oil

100 ml (3½ fl oz) full-fat milk

4 medium eggs

2 red onions, thinly sliced, to serve

In Kolkata in eastern India, Kathi Rolls are a staple food. Pancakes or parathas are filled with vegetables, cooked chicken or meat and then rolled up into a convenient sausage shape for easy handling.

1 Well ahead, make the filling by mixing together all the ingredients except the oil. Cover and leave to marinate for 2 hours in the refrigerator.

2 Soak 6 wooden skewers in cold water. Skewer the chicken and grill, barbecue, or bake at 180°C/350°F/ gas mark 4 for 20 minutes, until the chicken is cooked, basting with the remaining oil halfway through cooking.

3 To make the parathas, sift the flour and salt into a large bowl. Add the oil, milk and 1 egg, and knead for 7–10 minutes. Cover with a damp cloth and leave in a warm place for 20 minutes.

4 Divide the paratha mixture into 6 balls and on a floured surface roll each into a 16–17 cm (6½–7 inch) disc 5 mm (¼ inch) thick.

5 Beat together the remaining 3 eggs. Heat a frying pan. Put a paratha disc into the hot pan. After a minute, turn it over. Put 1–2 tablespoons of beaten egg on the paratha and spread it over the surface of the paratha. Immediately turn over the paratha again and cook the egged side for 30 seconds. Repeat with the rest of the paratha disks.

6 Put some cooked chicken in the centre of each paratha and roll up. Serve with onion slices and Dhaniyein ki Chatni (see page 126) mixed with yogurt.

Kashmiri Chicken Curry
Kashmiri Yakhani

SERVES 2−3

- 2 teaspoons fennel seeds
- 3 tablespoons groundnut or sunflower oil
- 5 green cardamoms
- 5–6 cloves
- 2–3 pieces of cinnamon, 5 cm (2 inches) in length
- 500 g (1 lb) lamb steaks, cut into 3 cm (1¼ inch) cubes
- ½ teaspoon salt
- ½ teaspoon ground ginger powder
- 200 ml (7 fl oz) natural yogurt, whipped
- ¼ teaspoon garam masala (see page 14)

Wazwan is a feast from Kashmir with many meat dishes in several courses and can consist of 40 dishes. The Yakhani is a sweet to mild curry that is very aromatic and generally made with yogurt and saffron.

1 Heat a frying pan and add the fennel seeds. After about 30 seconds when they start to release their aroma, remove them from the heat and allow to cool. Then place the fennel seeds in a pestle and mortar and grind to a fine powder. Set aside.

2 Heat the oil in a saucepan and tip in the cardamoms, cloves and cinnamon. Mix together and then add the lamb. Brown the meat over a medium to high heat for 12–15 minutes.

3 Add the salt, ground fennel and ginger powder to the lamb and mix well. Add 500 ml (17 fl oz) of hot water, cover and simmer for 25 minutes, or until the meat is tender.

4 Stir in the yogurt and let the curry cook for a further 2 minutes. Sprinkle the garam masala on top, then serve hot with Basmati Chawal (see page 124).

Black Pepper Chicken
Murgh Kaali Mirch

SERVES 6

3 tablespoons vegetable oil

1 teaspoon peeled and finely grated fresh root ginger

2 garlic cloves, crushed

¼ teaspoon salt

1 teaspoon coarsely ground black pepper

1 teaspoon ground white pepper

6 boneless and skinless chicken breasts, about 1 kg (2 lb), cut into bite-sized pieces

1 medium onion, finely chopped

2 green finger chillies, slit lengthways

1 teaspoon lemon juice

Besides chillies, the heat and pungency of pepper makes it a popular ingredient in curries. A couple of tablespoons of natural yogurt can be added to this recipe to reduce the power of the pepper.

1 Mix together 1 tablespoon of the oil, the ginger, garlic, salt and the black and white peppers, and rub the mixture into the chicken pieces. Cover and refrigerate for at least 30 minutes.

2 Heat the remaining oil in a wok and fry the onion for 2 minutes or until it is translucent. Add the marinated chicken pieces and gently stir-fry for 10 minutes until golden brown. Add the chillies and 200 ml (7 fl oz) boiling water, cover and simmer for 10 minutes or until the chicken is cooked.

3 To make a thicker or more concentrated sauce, remove the lid to let some of the water evaporate and continue cooking for another 5 minutes. Stir in the lemon juice just before serving.

4 Serve hot with Basmati Chawal (see page 124) and Aloo Gobhi (see page 72).

Fish

Fish Curry Cooked in Coconut
Meen Molee

3 garlic cloves

2 green finger chillies

5 cm (2 inch) square of fresh root ginger, peeled

3 tablespoons groundnut oil

1 small onion, thinly sliced

5–6 curry leaves (optional)

¼ teaspoon turmeric

¼ teaspoon salt

200 ml (7 fl oz) coconut milk

500 g (1 lb) haddock fillets, cut into 4 cm (1¾ inch) wide pieces

2 medium tomatoes, coarsely chopped

Meen Molee is a curry from Kerala in south India where fish is stewed in coconut milk. It is usually prepared with seerfish, but any white fish such as pollock, haddock or cod are just as good.

1 Mince the garlic, chillies and ginger together in a food processor.

2 Heat the oil in a frying pan or wok and fry the onion with the curry leaves (if using) for 4 minutes over a medium heat, or until the onion looks glazed.

3 Stir in the minced garlic mixture with the turmeric and salt. Fry for 2 minutes.

4 Add 100 ml (3½ fl oz) of the coconut milk with 150 ml (¼ pint) boiling water. Simmer for 2 minutes and then add the fish pieces and gently simmer for 5–6 minutes.

5 Add half the tomato and the remaining coconut milk and simmer for 3–4 minutes more.

6 Garnish with the remaining chopped tomato. Serve hot with Basmati Chawal (see page 124).

Spiced Prawns
Kolambi Masala

SERVES 2−3

2 tablespoons vegetable oil

½ medium white onion, finely chopped

3 garlic cloves, crushed

2 green finger chillies, finely chopped, or ¼ teaspoon hot chilli powder

15–20 raw prawns with shells

½ teaspoon tamarind concentrate or paste

pinch of asafoetida (optional)

pinch of hot chilli powder

¼ teaspoon salt

1 teaspoon ground cumin

½ teaspoon turmeric

1 teaspoon ground coriander

200 ml (7 fl oz) coconut milk

Maharashtrian cuisine contains hot and aromatic meat and fish curries and Kolambi Masala is a deliciously spiced and fiery thin sauce curry with prawns that is served as part of a main meal at lunchtime or in the evening. The prawns are shelled while eating.

1 Heat the oil in a heavy-based pan or wok. Gently fry the onion, garlic and green chillies (if using) for 2 minutes until the onion looks glazed. Add the prawns and stir-fry for 2 minutes. Remove from the heat.

2 Mix the tamarind paste with 2 tablespoons of cold water and leave for 2 minutes.

3 In a small bowl, mix together the asafoetida (if using), chilli powder, salt, cumin, turmeric and ground coriander with 2 tablespoons of cold water. Add this mixture to the prawns and stir for a minute.

4 Stir the diluted tamarind paste into the prawn mixture along with 250 ml (8 fl oz) boiling water. Simmer for 2 minutes, then add the coconut milk. Gently simmer for 6–8 minutes, but do not allow to boil.

5 Serve with Basmati Chawal (see page 124) and a mixed vegetable curry.

Five-spice Fish
Maacher Panch Phoran

SERVES 2

400 g (13 oz) sea bass, descaled, gutted and washed

¼ teaspoon salt

¼ teaspoon turmeric

2 tablespoons mustard oil

½ teaspoon panch phoran (see below)

2 green finger chillies, slit lengthways

FOR THE BATTA SHARSHEY (MUSTARD PASTE)

225 g (7½ oz) brown mustard seeds

FOR THE PANCH PHORAN (EAST INDIAN FIVE-SPICE MIX)

1 teaspoon fenugreek seeds, 1 teaspoon cumin seeds, 1 teaspoon fennel seeds, 1 teaspoon brown mustard seeds and 1 teaspoon nigella seeds, mixed together

As elsewhere in India, Bengalis eat everything with their fingers. This not only helps in the business of picking out treacherous fish bones, but it also increases the awareness of the texture of the food. You can use fish pieces or a whole fish in this recipe.

1 To make the batta sharshey, grind the mustard seeds to a fine powder with a pestle and mortar (3–4 minutes). Mix with equal quantities of cold water to use.

2 Cut several slits in the fish skin, then rub in the salt and the turmeric.

3 Heat the oil in a frying pan and fry the fish for 5 minutes, until golden, on both sides. Remove from the pan with a slotted spoon and set aside.

4 In the same oil, fry the panch phoran and chillies. Stir in 1 tablespoon of the batta sharshey and cook over a low heat for a minute. Return the fish to the pan and add 150 ml (¼ pint) boiling water. Cover and simmer for 5 minutes, until the sauce has thickened and the fish is cooked.

Amritsari Fish
Amritsari Macchi

SERVES 2−3

50 g (2 oz) besan or gram flour, sifted

1 tablespoon malt vinegar

1½ teaspoons hot chilli powder

1 garlic clove, crushed

1 teaspoon peeled and finely grated fresh root ginger

½ teaspoon ajowan seeds

1 teaspoon garam masala (see page 14)

½ teaspoon ground black pepper

½ teaspoon salt

1 tablespoon lemon juice

400 g (13 oz) boneless and skinless cod or sole fillets, in bite-size chunks

vegetable oil, for deep-frying

Though chicken is a favourite with non-vegetarians in particular across the whole of northern India, fish is also considered a delicacy, especially in the Amritsar region where the Sikh Golden Temple is situated. Chunky fish pieces are dipped in a blend of spices and herbs and then deep-fried.

1 In a bowl, mix the flour, vinegar, chilli powder, garlic, ginger, ajowan seeds, garam masala, black pepper and salt with 3 tablespoons of cold water to make a thick smooth batter.

2 Sprinkle the lemon juice over the fish, then place the fish pieces in the batter and carefully coat the fish, ensuring that the fish doesn't break up. Cover and leave to marinate for about 15 minutes.

3 Heat the oil in a deep-fryer or wok to 180°C/350°F. To check that the oil is at the right temperature, carefully add a small droplet of batter into the oil. If the batter sizzles, the oil is ready. Deep-fry the fish in batches. Cook for 8–10 minutes until golden brown, then drain on kitchen paper.

4 Serve immediately with Pudinay ki Chatni (see page 128).

Kerala Fish Curry

Eliya Mulakarachathu

SERVES 2-3

½ teaspoon hot chilli powder

5–6 shallots or 1 small onion, finely chopped

½ teaspoon turmeric

2 garlic cloves, roughly chopped

2 teaspoons peeled and finely grated fresh root ginger

¼ teaspoon salt

2 tablespoons groundnut oil

5–6 curry leaves

¼ teaspoon fenugreek seeds

pinch of brown or black mustard seeds

½ teaspoon tamarind concentrate or paste

500 g (1 lb) whole mackerel, descaled and gutted

This traditional fish curry from Kerala in the south of India is generally cooked in an earthenware vessel known as a chatti, which adds to the flavour. It is usually made with coconut oil but works well with groundnut oil.

1 Place the chilli powder, shallots or onion, half the turmeric, the garlic, ginger and salt in a blender and blitz to a fine paste. Alternatively, use a pestle and mortar.

2 Heat the oil in a large frying pan and add the curry leaves, fenugreek and mustard seeds. When the seeds have popped, add the spice paste and cook gently over a low heat, stirring occasionally, for 4 minutes.

3 In a small bowl, mix the tamarind with 4 tablespoons cold water, then add to the pan and stir in.

4 Wash the mackerel and pat dry with kitchen paper. Cut 3–4 diagonal slits on each side of the fish and season with the remaining turmeric.

5 Carefully add the fish to the pan, nose to tail, cover and simmer for 10 minutes on a low heat or until the sauce thickens and the fish is cooked. For extra sauce, stir in 3 tablespoons boiling water and simmer briefly.

6 Serve hot with Basmati Chawal (see page 124).

Marathi Salmon Curry
Kaalvan

SERVES 2–3

2 tablespoons
   groundnut or
   vegetable oil

2–3 garlic cloves, lightly
   crushed

250 g (8 oz) salmon
   fillets or skinned and
   boned salmon steaks

1 teaspoon rice flour or
   plain flour

1 teaspoon hot chilli
   powder

½ teaspoon turmeric

1 teaspoon ground
   cumin

1 teaspoon ground
   coriander

½ teaspoon salt

½ teaspoon tamarind
   concentrate or paste

200 ml (7 fl oz) coconut
   milk

Maharashtrians call curry or any dish with a sauce base, Kaalvan. The interesting thing about this curry is that it has no onions. The full flavours of the curry can be appreciated with just plain basmati rice.

1 Heat the oil in a heavy-based pan. Add the garlic and fish. Fry each side of the steaks over a low heat for 4–5 minutes until lightly browned.

2 In a bowl, mix together all the other ingredients, except the coconut milk, with 150 ml (¼ pint) cold water. Add to the pan and simmer for 3 minutes.

3 Mix the coconut milk with 100 ml (3½ fl oz) boiling water and add to the pan, cover and simmer for 7 minutes: the sauce should be quite runny.

4 Serve hot with Chawlichi Bhaji (see page 94).

Creamy Prawn Curry
Chingri Malai Jhol

SERVES 2−3

¼ teaspoon salt

½ teaspoon turmeric

500 g (1 lb) peeled and cooked small prawns

1 teaspoon peeled and roughly chopped fresh root ginger

2 garlic cloves, roughly chopped

1 small onion, roughly chopped

3 tablespoons mustard oil or groundnut oil

1 bay leaf (optional)

¼ teaspoon hot chilli powder

200 ml (7 fl oz) coconut milk

pinch of garam masala (optional, see page 14)

pinch of mild chilli powder

With the Bay of Bengal to the south of the state of West Bengal, it is not surprising that fish is central to the region's cooking. They have a fondness for shellfish too, especially prawns, which are often cooked in mildly spiced coconut milk.

1 Sprinkle the salt and turmeric over the prawns, toss gently and set aside.

2 Blitz the ginger, garlic and onion into a coarse paste in a blender.

3 Heat the oil in a large heavy-based pan or wok and tip in the prawns. Fry over a medium heat for 5 minutes. Remove the prawns with a slotted spoon and set aside.

4 Place the bay leaf (if using) in the pan and allow it to sizzle. Add the ginger paste and fry for 6–8 minutes over a medium heat. Mix in the hot chilli powder, then stir in the fried prawns, followed by the coconut milk. Allow it to cook for a minute until piping hot – do not let it boil – then mix in the garam masala (if using) and remove from the heat. If you like more sauce, add 200 ml (7 fl oz) boiling water with the coconut milk, and gently simmer for 3–4 minutes to thicken.

5 Garnish with mild chilli powder and serve hot.

Bengali Fish Curry
Doi Maach

SERVES 2—3

400 g (13 oz) skinless and boneless white fish fillets, cut into 5 cm (2 inch) pieces

½ teaspoon turmeric

½ teaspoon salt

3 tablespoons groundnut or sunflower oil

3 bay leaves

3–4 dried red chillies

½ teaspoon nigella or onion seeds

1 onion, finely chopped

¼ teaspoon chilli powder

½ teaspoon ground coriander

½ teaspoon ground cumin

1 teaspoon peeled and grated fresh root ginger

Nigella seeds, often known as onion seeds, are one of the ingredients of paanch phoran, which is the Bengali five-spice mixture. Once heated, they impart a nutty yet bittersweet flavour and can also be found sprinkled on naans or leavened breads.

1 Rub the fish fillets with the turmeric and salt.

2 Heat the oil in a frying pan and fry the fish over a medium heat for 7–10 minutes or until lightly browned. Remove the fish from the pan and set aside.

3 To the same pan, add the bay leaves, dried red chillies, nigella or onion seeds and mix. Tip in the onion and fry for 5–7 minutes.

4 Mix the chilli powder, coriander, cumin and ginger with 6 tablespoons water. Pour the spice mixture into the pan and add the fried fish. Simmer for 5 minutes. If you want more sauce, add 3 tablespoons of extra water to the pan and cook for a further 2 minutes.

5 Serve hot.

Fish Curry
Maacher Jhol

SERVES 3–4

½ teaspoon turmeric

1 teaspoon ground cumin

1 teaspoon ground coriander

2 green finger chillies, chopped

¼ teaspoon salt

30 g (1 oz) coriander leaves, chopped

500 g (1 lb) hoki or haddock fillets, skinned and cut into pieces 7–8 cm (3–3½ inches) long

3 tablespoons groundnut oil

¼ teaspoon cumin seeds

½ teaspoon brown or black mustard seeds

2 garlic cloves, crushed

1 teaspoon peeled and grated fresh root ginger

1 medium onion, finely chopped

2 medium tomatoes, roughly chopped

A typical Bengali fish curry, Maacher Jhol is a light fish stew, seasoned with ground and whole spices. The sauce is thin yet packed with flavour. Whole green chillies are usually added at the end of the cooking.

1 Mix together the turmeric, ground cumin, ground coriander, chillies, salt and 20 g (¾ oz) of the coriander leaves. Coat the fish evenly with this spice mixture.

2 Heat 2 tablespoons of the oil in a frying pan. Fry the fish for 2 minutes on each side or until lightly browned. Drain on kitchen paper and set aside.

3 Heat the remaining oil in the same pan and add the cumin and mustard seeds. When they pop, add the garlic, ginger, onion and tomatoes. Fry gently for 8 minutes.

4 Add 200 ml (7 fl oz) boiling water and stir for a minute. Return the fish to the pan and simmer for 10–12 minutes or until the sauce is brownish and not too thick and the fish is cooked.

5 Garnish with the remaining coriander leaves and serve hot with Basmati Chawal (see page 124) and Chholar Dal (see page 113).

Prawns with Coconut
Thenga Kuda Eraal

SERVES 4

½ teaspoon tamarind
concentrate or paste

½ teaspoon hot chilli
powder

1 teaspoon ground
cumin

½ teaspoon turmeric

¼ teaspoon salt

1 tablespoon groundnut
or vegetable oil

1 garlic clove, sliced

12 king prawns, cooked,
shelled and deveined

½ teaspoon peeled and
finely grated fresh
root ginger

1 green finger chilli,
finely chopped
(optional)

100 ml (3½ fl oz)
coconut cream

2 tablespoons roughly
chopped coriander
leaves

Prawns are popular in the south of India and partner the ubiquitous coconut very well, inspiring many recipes. The use of tamarind in this dish balances the sweetness of the coconut.

1 In a bowl, mix 2 tablespoons of cold water, the tamarind, chilli powder, cumin, turmeric and salt.

2 Heat the oil in a heavy-based pan over a medium heat. Add the garlic and prawns, and sauté for 2 minutes. Stir in the ginger, green chilli (if using) and tamarind mixture. Add 100 ml (3½ fl oz) boiling water and simmer for 2 minutes.

3 Carefully add the coconut cream because it tends to spit. Simmer for 3 minutes, then stir in the coriander leaves.

4 Serve immediately with Basmati Chawal (see page 124).

Pickled Prawns
Balchão de Camarão

SERVES 2-3

- 2 teaspoons peeled and finely grated fresh root ginger
- 2 garlic cloves, roughly chopped
- 4 dried medium red chillies, stalks removed
- 1 tablespoon malt vinegar
- 2 cloves
- ¼ teaspoon brown or black mustard seeds or ¼ teaspoon mustard powder (optional)
- ½ teaspoon ground cumin
- ¼ teaspoon salt
- ¼ teaspoon ground cinnamon
- ½ teaspoon turmeric
- 2 tablespoons groundnut oil or vegetable oil
- 175 g (6 oz) raw king prawns, shelled and deveined
- 4–6 curry leaves
- 1 small white onion, finely chopped
- 2 medium tomatoes, finely chopped

chilli powder, to serve

Balchão de Camarão is a Goan recipe in which the prawns are cooked in a brine sauce. Often vegetables such as aubergines are also 'pickled' in sugar, vinegar and spices for a day or two before eating. The tangier the better.

1 In a food processor, mince together the ginger, garlic, chillies, vinegar, cloves, mustard seeds or powder (if using), cumin, salt, ground cinnamon and turmeric to form a smooth paste.

2 Heat 1 tablespoon of oil in a wok or a saucepan and sauté the prawns for 5 minutes until all the water has evaporated. Remove the prawns with a slotted spoon, drain on kitchen paper and set aside.

3 In the same pan, add the remaining oil followed by the curry leaves. Stir in the onion and fry over a medium heat for 6 minutes until golden.

4 Add the tomatoes to the fried onions and cook for about 2 minutes. Stir in the ginger paste and gently fry for 2 minutes. Add 2 tablespoons of cold water to the food processor to rinse and add this water to the pan. Return the prawns to the pan and simmer for a further 3 minutes.

5 Serve hot or cold, sprinkled with a pinch of chilli powder.

Vegetables

Vegetable Biryani
Subz Biryani

SERVES 4

75 g (3 oz) butter or ghee, plus more for greasing

200 g (7 oz) white basmati rice

1 onion, sliced

2 x 5 cm (2 inch) pieces of cassia bark or cinnamon

6 cloves

2 bay leaves

1 teaspoon cumin seeds

150 g (5 oz) green peas, defrosted if frozen

150 g (5 oz) green beans, topped and tailed, and cut into 3 cm (1¼ inch) pieces

150 g (5 oz) cauliflower florets

4 garlic cloves, crushed

¼ teaspoon salt

½ teaspoon chilli powder

250 ml (8 fl oz) natural yogurt, whipped

4 tablespoons full-fat or semi-skimmed milk

a few saffron strands

Biryanis are predominantly made with meat. However, the whole spices in this recipe would complement any sort of vegetable incredibly well. This is my favourite combination of vegetables.

1 Preheat the oven to 180°C/350°F/gas mark 4 and grease a large ovenproof casserole with a tight-fitting lid.

2 Rinse the rice thoroughly in cold running water and place in a pan with 400 ml (14 fl oz) boiling water. Cover and boil for 8 minutes or until the rice is half-cooked. The grains should be soft on the outside but still hard in the centre.

3 While the rice is cooking, melt the butter or ghee in a saucepan and fry the onion for 5 minutes or until crisp and golden brown. Remove the onion from the pan and set aside.

4 Add to the pan the cassia bark or cinnamon, cloves, bay leaves and cumin seeds and fry for 30 seconds to 1 minute or until you can smell their aroma. Tip in the vegetables and continue frying for 5 minutes, stirring occasionally. Add the garlic, salt, chilli powder and yogurt, and mix in.

5 Gently warm the milk in a small saucepan and soak the saffron strands in it for a few minutes.

6 Place a layer of the vegetables on the base of the casserole and cover it with a layer of rice and a few saffron strands along with the milk. Repeat the layers until all the ingredients have been used, ending with a top layer of rice.

7 Cover and bake for 25 minutes, or until the biryani is heated through.

8 Serve hot with Tadka Raita (see page 131).

Kashmiri Spinach
Kashmiri Palak

SERVES 2-3

3 tablespoons sunflower or vegetable oil

pinch of asafoetida

250 g (8 oz) spinach leaves

¼ teaspoon turmeric

¼ teaspoon chilli powder

¼ teaspoon salt

¼ teaspoon Kashmiri garam masala (below) or garam masala (see page 14)

1 teaspoon peeled and finely grated fresh root ginger

FOR THE KASHMIRI GARAM MASALA

3-4 bay leaves

2 star anise

2-3 cinnamon sticks or cassia bark pieces

1 tablespoon black cumin seeds (shahi jeera)

5-6 green cardamoms, seeds only

8 black cardamoms, seeds only

¼ teaspoon cloves

1 teaspoon black peppercorns

½ a nutmeg

Dishes made with greens in India are often prepared using spinach, mustard leaves and other greens, which are then cooked with ground spices almost until it is in a mushy state. This recipe makes the most of seasonal spinach and the cooking time is greatly reduced.

1 To make the Kashmiri garam masala, heat a frying pan and add all the ingredients. Stir for 10 seconds to release the aromas. Remove from the heat, then grind the mixture in a coffee mill, or using a pestle and mortar, to a fine or medium-fine powder. Sieve the powder to get rid of any fibres. Store in an airtight container away from sunlight for up to 3-6 months. Use, sprinkling sparingly, at the end of cooking.

2 Heat the oil in a wok or saucepan and add the asafoetida. When it sizzles, tip in the spinach and fry for 5 minutes until wilted. Add the turmeric, chilli powder and salt, and cook for 3 minutes more.

3 Add the Kashmiri garam masala or garam masala and mix in with the ginger. Serve hot.

Seasoned Potato and Cauliflower
Aloo Gobhi

SERVES 2 – 3

200 g (7 oz) cauliflower florets, cut into 4 cm (1¾ inch) pieces

2 tablespoons vegetable or groundnut oil

1 large onion, finely chopped

2 green finger chillies, finely chopped

2 garlic cloves, finely chopped

300 g (10 oz) white potatoes, peeled and cut into 2 cm (⅘ inch) cubes

1 teaspoon turmeric

¼ teaspoon ground cumin

¼ teaspoon ground coriander

½ teaspoon salt

¼ teaspoon garam masala (see page 14)

1 tablespoon butter or ghee

1 teaspoon peeled and finely grated fresh root ginger

Go to any home in the north of India during the winter months and the proverbial Aloo Gobhi will be served at least once a week, either as an accompaniment to a curry or as the main dish with chapatis.

1 Wash the cauliflower well in salted cold water.

2 Heat the oil in a frying pan and add the onion, chillies, garlic and potatoes, and fry for 7 minutes or until the onion is deep yellow and translucent.

3 Add the cauliflower and fry for a further 3 minutes until light brown. Add the turmeric, cumin, coriander, salt and garam masala, stir and fry gently for 5 minutes. Mix well. Add the butter and mix, then add 5 tablespoons of cold water, cover and simmer for 5 minutes. Stir in the ginger.

4 Serve hot with Dal Makhani (see page 125).

Regal Indian Cheese
Shahi Paneer

SERVES 2–3

3 tablespoons vegetable oil

½ teaspoon cumin seeds

2 black cardamoms, seeds only

1 medium onion, finely chopped

2 garlic cloves, crushed

1 teaspoon peeled and grated fresh root ginger

2 green finger chillies, finely chopped

200 g (7 oz) plum tomatoes, blended until smooth

2 tablespoons natural unsweetened yogurt

1 teaspoon cornflour

1 teaspoon tomato purée

1 teaspoon demerara sugar

¼ teaspoon salt

pinch of garam masala (see page 14)

pinch of medium-hot chilli powder

250 g (8 oz) paneer, cut into 2.5 cm (1 inch) cubes

2 tablespoons double cream

handful of coriander leaves, chopped

Shahi means royal or regal and Shahi cuisine is the food of the Mogul kings who conquered parts of India. The distinctive ingredients in Shahi dishes are lots of dairy-based products such as cream, butter, yogurt and paneer.

1 Heat the oil in a heavy-based pan, then stir in the cumin and black cardamom seeds. Fry for 30 seconds, then add the onion, garlic, ginger and green chillies. Fry for 3 minutes or until the onions are lightly browned. Tip in the tomatoes and cook for a further 4 minutes or until the sauce is thick and creamy. Gradually fold in the yogurt.

2 Remove the mixture from the heat. Mix the cornflour and 2 tablespoons of cold water together to make a smooth paste and then stir into the onion mixture. Return the pan to the heat, add the tomato purée, sugar and 4 tablespoons of cold water, and stir. Tip in the salt, garam masala and chilli powder. Stir in the paneer and cook on a low heat for 2 minutes. Swirl in the double cream and cook for a minute longer.

3 Garnish with coriander to serve.

Spiced Green Beans
Hari Phali Subzi

SERVES 2–3

2 tablespoons sunflower or vegetable oil

1 small onion, finely chopped

¼ teaspoon turmeric

¼ teaspoon chilli powder

½ teaspoon ground cumin

¼ teaspoon salt

1 teaspoon tomato purée

200 g (7 oz) fine beans, topped, tailed and chopped into 2.5 cm (1 inch) lengths

Green beans are a vegetable that can work well with any spice. This dish makes a handsome partner to a main curry dish and contains very little sauce. It can be eaten on its own with chapatis.

1 Heat a frying pan and add the oil. Tip in the onion and fry for 3–4 minutes until golden brown.

2 Add the turmeric, chilli powder, cumin and salt. Mix for a minute, add the tomato purée, followed by the green beans and fry for a further 2 minutes.

3 Pour in 100 ml (3½ fl oz) water. Cook for 3–4 minutes until the beans are tender.

4 Serve hot.

Savoury Lentil Pancakes
Chila

MAKES 10

250 g (8 oz) moong dal

2.5 cm (1 inch) piece of fresh root ginger, peeled and grated

1–2 small green chillies, finely chopped

¼ teaspoon asafoetida

¼ teaspoon turmeric

1 onion, finely chopped

2 tablespoons finely chopped coriander leaves

½ teaspoon salt

sunflower or vegetable oil, for frying

Asafoetida is a dried yellow resin obtained from the roots of a fennel plant. Its a spice generally used with lentil dishes to ease the digestion of heavy lentils and pulses. This dish is eaten at breakfast, often with a green mint and coriander chutney.

1 Rinse the dal well and place in a bowl. Pour in 3 cupfuls of cold water (enough to immerse the dal) and leave to soak for 2–3 hours.

2 Drain the dal, reserving 125 ml (4 fl oz) of the water. Add the ginger, chillies, asafoetida and turmeric to the water. Blitz the water and spices in a blender or with an electric hand whisk to make a smooth batter. Pour the batter into a bowl and add the onion, coriander leaves and salt. Mix well.

3 Heat a frying pan, add a teaspoon of oil and tilt the pan to coat. Drop a tablespoon of batter in the centre of the pan. Using the back of a ladle, spread the batter into a circle about 10 cm (4 inches) in diameter. Fry for 2–3 minutes on each side until brown spots appear on the surface. Taste one chila to see if the batter needs any more seasoning and then make the rest of the chilas with the remaining batter.

Okra from Jaipur
Bhindi Jaipuri

SERVES 4

250 g (8 oz) okra

50 g (2 oz) gram flour
(besan)

½ teaspoon ground
cumin

½ teaspoon turmeric

½ teaspoon chilli
powder

½ teaspoon mango
powder (amchur)

½ teaspoon salt

¼ teaspoon nigella or
onion seeds

sunflower oil, for
deep-frying

Okra or ladies fingers are an acquired taste but they are an extremely versatile vegetable, used in dry savoury Indian dishes. This dish is a popular teatime snack and can also be eaten as an accompaniment to a meat curry.

1 Wash the okra and dry thoroughly. Cut off the stalks. Slice the pods at an angle into 3 cm (1¼ inch) pieces. Place the gram flour in a bowl and add the cumin, turmeric, chilli powder, mango powder, salt and nigella seeds. Mix well and fold in the okra pieces. Add 3–4 teaspoons of water to make a thick and sticky paste.

2 Heat the oil in a deep-fryer or wok to 180°C/350°F. To check that the oil is at the right temperature, carefully add a small droplet of the okra mixture to the oil; if the mixture sizzles, the oil is ready. Carefully drop in a tablespoon of okra at a time into the oil. Fry the okra pieces for 3–5 minutes or until they are golden. Remove and drain on kitchen paper.

3 Serve immediately with Phulkas (see page 106) or Basmati Chawal (see page 124) and a tomato chutney.

Cauliflower Fritters
Gobhi Pakora

SERVES 2 – 3

400 g (14 oz) cauliflower florets, cut into 2.5 cm (1 inch) pieces

200 g (7 oz) gram flour

½ teaspoon coriander seeds, crushed

½ teaspoon ground cumin

½ teaspoon salt

½ teaspoon turmeric

½ teaspoon medium-hot chilli powder

pinch of baking powder

vegetable oil, for deep-frying

Pakoras, north Indian appetizers or snacks, are batter-fried vegetables or fish. The batter is usually made of gram flour (besan) mixed with water and a few select spices such as coriander and chilli.

1 Wash the cauliflower thoroughly in salted cold water.

2 Whisk the gram flour and 250 ml (8 fl oz) cold water together with the coriander seeds, cumin, salt, turmeric, chilli powder and baking powder, until it becomes a smooth runny paste.

3 Heat oil in a deep-fryer or wok to 180°C/350°F. To check that the oil is at the right temperature, carefully add a small droplet of batter to the oil; if the batter sizzles, the oil is ready.

4 Tip the cauliflower florets into the batter, coat thoroughly, then lift out with a slotted spoon and carefully immerse them in the hot oil. Fry in batches for 3 minutes or until they are golden brown. Remove and drain on kitchen paper.

5 Serve immediately with Pudinay ki Chatni (see page 128).

Vegetarian Kebabs
Hara Bhara Kabab

MAKES 6 – 8
KABABS

125 g (4 oz) **spinach leaves, finely chopped**

125 g (4 oz) **white or red potatoes, peeled and boiled**

125 g (4 oz) **green peas, cooked**

2 **green finger chillies, finely chopped**

1 **teaspoon peeled and finely grated fresh root ginger**

½ **teaspoon salt**

2 **tablespoons roughly chopped coriander leaves**

3 **tablespoons cornflour**

4 **tablespoons vegetable oil**

Kababs are usually made with meat, fish or chicken. These have evolved from the Mogul-style kababs and been adapted for the vegetarian market. 'Hara bhara' means 'laden with greens or vegetables'.

1 Wash the spinach thoroughly in salted cold water.

2 In a large bowl mix together the potatoes, peas, spinach, chillies, ginger, salt, coriander leaves and cornflour. Mash until smooth.

3 Take a spoonful of mixture roughly the size of a golf ball and flatten to make a burger shape. Repeat with the remaining mixture.

4 Heat the oil in a heavy-based frying pan and shallow-fry the kababs for 2 minutes on each side, cooking them well. Drain on kitchen paper.

5 Serve hot with Tadka Raita (see page 131).

Aubergines in a Tamarind Sauce
Keralan Brinjals

SERVES 4

500 g (1 lb) small purple aubergines or 8–10 small aubergines

1 teaspoon salt

2 tablespoons tamarind pulp

3 tablespoons groundnut or sunflower oil

½ teaspoon brown or black mustard seeds

8–10 curry leaves

1 onion, finely chopped

1 teaspoon ground cumin

1 teaspoon ground coriander

½ teaspoon chilli powder

½ teaspoon turmeric

3–4 garlic cloves, crushed

5 cm (2 inch) piece of fresh root ginger, peeled and grated

50 g (2 oz) creamed coconut

a few chopped coriander leaves to garnish

When buying aubergines, make sure they have a smooth surface and are light – the heavier ones contain too many seeds. Apparently salting aubergines, which isn't really necessary anymore, makes them absorb less oil when cooked.

1 Make 2 crossing slits on the bulbous end of each of the aubergines and place in a bowl. Sprinkle ½ teaspoon of salt over them and set aside.

2 Place the tamarind pulp in a small bowl and add 4 tablespoons of hot water. Leave to stand for 10 minutes. Use a wooden spoon to press the pulp and release the seeds, if any, and fibres. Then strain this through a nylon sieve into a bowl, pressing with the back of a spoon to extract as much juice as possible. Reserve the juice but discard the pulp.

3 Heat the oil in a large saucepan or a deep wok and add a few mustard seeds. The seeds will splutter when the oil is hot enough. Add the remaining mustard seeds followed by the curry leaves and stir.

4 Add the onion and fry for 2–3 minutes until the onion turns translucent. Add the cumin, coriander, chilli powder, turmeric and the remaining salt, and mix. Then add the garlic, ginger and aubergines. Pour in 200 ml (7 fl oz) of just boiled water along with the tamarind juice, stir, cover and simmer for 10 minutes.

5 Fold in the coconut cream and cook for a further 2 minutes. Serve hot, garnished with coriander leaves, accompanied by Basmati Chawal (see page 124).

Vegetables in Coconut
Avial

500 g (1 lb) mixed
vegetables (courgettes,
green bananas,
Brussel sprouts cut
into 2.5 cm/1 inch
pieces; peeled
potatoes cut into
1.25 cm/½ inch cubes;
sliced carrots and
aubergines; and
trimmed green beans)

pinch of turmeric

1½ teaspoons ground
cumin

4 green finger chillies,
chopped

125 g (4 oz) grated fresh
coconut

1 medium onion,
chopped

½ teaspoon salt

1 tablespoon
unsweetened
natural yogurt

¼ teaspoon tamarind
concentrate or paste

8–10 curry leaves, to
serve

Avial is a thick, mixed vegetable dish in which the vegetables are chopped and parboiled, flavoured with yogurt and then cooked in coconut milk. Avial also forms part of a vegetarian feast in Kerala known as the 'sadya'.

1 Place all the vegetables in a heavy-based pan. Add 250 ml (8 fl oz) boiling water and the turmeric and simmer for 5–10 minutes or until the vegetables are tender.

2 Meanwhile, in a pestle and mortar or blender, grind together the cumin, green chillies, 100 g (3½ oz) of the grated coconut, the onion, salt and 6 tablespoons of cold water to make a coarse paste. Add the paste and yogurt to the cooked vegetables and stir. Lower the heat and simmer for 2 minutes. Stir in the tamarind and simmer for 4 minutes more.

3 Garnish with the curry leaves and remaining grated coconut and serve hot.

Potato and Egg Curry
Aloo Dimer Jhol

SERVES 2

- 2 white or red potatoes, peeled and cut into 4 cm (1¾ inch) cubes
- 2 tablespoons mustard oil or groundnut oil
- 4 medium eggs, hard-boiled and shelled
- 1 teaspoon turmeric
- 1 small onion, finely chopped
- 1 green finger chilli, finely chopped
- 1 teaspoon peeled and finely grated fresh root ginger
- ¼ teaspoon garam masala (see page 14)
- ½ teaspoon ground cumin
- ¼ teaspoon salt
- sprig of coriander leaves, finely chopped (optional)

East Indians cook many dishes with potatoes. Dimer means egg in Bengali and several fried-egg style dishes, such as this one, are made for breakfast. It usually has a lot of sauce, which is soaked up with plain basmati rice.

1 Parboil the potatoes for 10 minutes. Drain.

2 Heat the oil in a heavy-based pan and fry the potatoes over a medium heat for 4 minutes or until golden brown. Remove from the pan with a slotted spoon and set aside.

3 Make 2 small slits on the eggs and fill with the turmeric. Fry the eggs for 2 minutes or until golden, then remove from the pan.

4 Place the onion in the pan and sauté over a medium heat for 3 minutes or until golden brown. Add the chilli and ginger and fry for a minute. Add the garam masala and cumin and stir-fry for a minute. Add the potatoes and salt. Mix well, then pour in 200 ml (7 fl oz) boiling water and bring to the boil. Add the eggs and sauté over a medium heat for 6–7 minutes or until golden brown.

5 Garnish with coriander leaves (if using) and serve hot with Basmati Chawal (see page 124).

Small Dishes &
Accompaniments

Sweet and Sour Potatoes
Aloo Chaat

SERVES 4

FOR THE DATE
AND TAMARIND
CHUTNEY

- 50 g (2 oz) dried dates, stoned and chopped
- 1 tablespoon tamarind concentrate
- ¼ teaspoon salt
- ¼ teaspoon chilli powder
- 1 teaspoon groundnut or sunflower oil

FOR THE GREEN
CHUTNEY

- 25 g (1 oz) coriander leaves, roughly chopped
- 4 green finger chillies, roughly chopped
- 1 garlic clove, crushed
- 1 teaspoon peeled and finely grated fresh root ginger
- 4 mint leaves (optional)
- ¼ teaspoon salt

FOR THE POTATO
MIXTURE

- 3 tablespoons groundnut or sunflower oil
- 400 g (13 oz) potatoes, peeled, boiled and chopped into 2.5 cm (1 inch) cubes
- ½ teaspoon cumin seeds
- ¼ teaspoon chilli powder
- ¼ teaspoon salt
- 4 tablespoons yogurt, whipped

Chaat is a collection of savoury Indian snacks often served as street food in Indian cities and there are variations from region to region. Most contain tamarind and deep-fried wheat snacks seasoned with a green chutney.

1 First make the date and tamarind chutney: in a blender, blitz all the ingredients with 4 tablespoons of cold water to make a fairly smooth paste.

2 In the same way, make the green chutney: in a blender, blitz all the ingredients with 4 tablespoons of cold water to make a fairly smooth paste.

3 For the potato mixture: heat the oil in a frying pan and sauté the potatoes for 7–8 minutes until browned at the edges. Drain on kitchen paper and set aside.

4 Wipe the frying pan of excess oil with kitchen paper and add the cumin seeds. Dry-fry them for a minute until you can smell their aroma. Allow them to cool, then place in a pestle and mortar and grind to a fine powder.

5 Divide the potatoes between serving plates and sprinkle a little of the ground cumin seeds over each, followed by the chilli powder and salt. Then add a tablespoon of yogurt to each plate and top with a teaspoon each of date and tamarind chutney and the green chutney.

Maharashtrian Radish Salad
Mooli Chi Koshimbir

SERVES 2-3

150 g (5 oz) radishes, topped and tailed

1 small white onion, finely chopped

½ teaspoon salt

1 green finger chilli, finely chopped

2 medium tomatoes, finely chopped

2 teaspoons lemon juice

30 g (1 oz) coriander leaves, roughly chopped

'Koshimbir' in Marathi (the language commonly spoken in Maharashtra where Mumbai is the capital) means salad. Indians tend not to make elaborate dressings that include oil. This is a quick salad with a simple dressing of lemon juice and salt, the main flavours coming from the chilli and the coriander.

1 Coarsely grate the radishes and mix with the rest of the ingredients.

2 Serve as a fresh relish with any fish curry, such as Kaalvan (see page 58), or a mixed vegetable curry and Kolambi Masala (see page 52).

Cucumber Yogurt Salad
Vellarikka Pachadi

SERVES 4

155 ml (5½ fl oz) natural unsweetened yogurt

½ teaspoon ground cumin

1 tablespoon finely chopped coriander leaves

¼ teaspoon salt

1 medium cucumber, roughly grated

1 teaspoon sunflower oil

2 green finger chillies, slit lengthways

1 tablespoon unsalted peanuts, crushed (optional)

This is a variety of yogurt salad seasoned with chilli and cumin, which can be served with a lentil dish and chapatis.

1 Whisk the yogurt until it is smooth. Mix in the cumin, coriander leaves and salt.

2 Squeeze out as much water as you can from the grated cucumber and fold into the yogurt.

3 Heat the oil in a small frying pan. Add the chillies and peanuts (if using). Fry for a minute, then set aside to cool for a couple of minutes.

4 Mix well with the yogurt and chill for at least 30 minutes before serving.

Marathi Black-eyed Beans
Chawlichi Bhaji

SERVES 4

275 g (9 oz) dried black-eyed beans

2 tablespoons vegetable oil

¼ teaspoon brown or black mustard seeds

1 small white onion, finely chopped

2 green finger chillies, chopped

pinch of asafoetida (optional)

1 medium tomato, roughly chopped

½ teaspoon salt

handful of coriander leaves, roughly chopped

Black-eyed beans are a staple in Maharashtra and Gujarat in western India, and are braised with spices in stews and other dishes. This is a dish that is served as part of a main meal in a thali or on a plate.

1 Pick over the beans to check for small stones, then place in a sieve and rinse under cold running water. Soak the beans in 750 ml (1¼ pints) cold water for an hour.

2 Drain and place in a saucepan with 500 ml (17 fl oz) cold water. Boil for 45 minutes. Drain.

3 Heat the oil in a heavy-based pan. Tip in the mustard seeds. When they begin to pop, add the onion, chillies and asafoetida (if using) and gently fry for 3 minutes. Then add the chopped tomato, beans and salt, and fry over a medium heat for 2 minutes. Cover and simmer for a further 5 minutes.

4 Sprinkle with coriander leaves and serve hot with Kaalvan (see page 58) and Basmati Chawal (see page 124).

Chickpeas with Spinach
Chana Palak

SERVES 3-4

4 tablespoons sunflower oil

2 bay leaves

1 piece of cassia bark, or cinnamon stick, 5–6 cm (2–2½ inches) long

2 onions, finely chopped

3–4 garlic cloves, chopped

5 cm (2 inch) piece of fresh root ginger, peeled and chopped

½ teaspoon turmeric

1 teaspoon ground cumin

1 teaspoon ground coriander

1 teaspoon mango powder (amchur) or 1 teaspoon lemon juice

¼ teaspoon chilli powder

½ teaspoon salt

½ teaspoon garam masala (see page 14)

400 g (13 oz) cooked chickpeas

1 large bunch of spinach or 2 handfuls of baby spinach leaves, rinsed

If you're using dried chickpeas, make sure they are soaked in water for at least eight hours before cooking them. This dish is ideal as an accompaniment or even a main vegetarian dish.

1 Heat the oil in a heavy-based saucepan and add the bay leaves and cassia bark. Mix for 30 seconds until they start to sizzle and you can smell the aroma of the spices.

2 Add the onions and fry for 7 minutes until the mixture turns light brown.

3 Add the garlic and ginger into the pan along with the turmeric, cumin, coriander, mango powder or lemon juice, chilli powder, salt and garam masala, and fry for 2 minutes. Tip in the chickpeas and fry for 5 minutes while mashing some of the chickpeas. Add 6 tablespoons of water and simmer for 7–8 minutes.

4 Reduce to a low heat, add the spinach and cover. Allow the spinach to wilt for 2–4 minutes.

5 Serve hot with Phulkas (see page 106).

Spicy Okra
Masala Bhindi

SERVES 2–3

250 g (8 oz) okra

3 tablespoons sunflower or vegetable oil

1 onion, sliced

3–4 garlic cloves, sliced

2 green chillies, chopped

½ teaspoon salt

¼ teaspoon turmeric

½ teaspoon ground coriander

½ teaspoon ground cumin

Although okra originated in Africa, Indians have embraced this vegetable by making all kinds of savoury dishes with it. When buying okra or ladies fingers, choose smaller pods as large ones tend to be more fibrous.

1 Slice off the tops of the okra and discard. Slice the rest into little rounds about 1.5cm (¾ inch) thick.

2 Heat the oil in a frying pan and fry the onion, garlic and chillies for 2 minutes. Then tip in the okra, salt, turmeric, coriander and cumin, and continue to fry for 7–9 minutes, stirring regularly to make sure the okra does not burn.

3 Serve hot with Phulkas (see page 106).

Fried Aubergine
Begun Bhaja

SERVES 2

1 medium aubergine

1 teaspoon salt

½ teaspoon turmeric

3 tablespoons mustard oil or vegetable oil

small handful of coriander leaves, roughly chopped

Like many east Indian recipes, this one is very simple, using just one key spice.

1 Remove the stem from the aubergine, then cut in lengthways in four before cutting each length in half. You should end up with eight pieces.

2 Rub the cut surfaces of the aubergine with salt and turmeric and set aside for 30 minutes.

3 Heat the oil in a frying pan and shallow-fry on a low-to-medium heat for 5 minutes on each side until golden brown. Garnish with coriander leaves.

Unleavened Fenugreek Flatbread
Thepla

MAKES 6

150 g (5 oz) wholemeal flour, plus more for dusting

¼ teaspoon turmeric

pinch of asafoetida (optional)

20–30 g (¾–1½ oz) fenugreek leaves, finely chopped, or 2 tablespoons dried

½ teaspoon mild chilli powder

½ teaspoon ground coriander

½ teaspoon cumin seeds

¼ teaspoon peeled and finely grated fresh root ginger

3 tablespoons vegetable or groundnut oil

Theplas are Gujarati baked flatbreads, and are similar to chapatis. The dough is made with wheat flour, often mixed with gram flour or besan, and fresh fenugreek leaves. Many Gujaratis avoid eating garlic for religious reasons, so this is one of many recipes from the region that does not contain it.

1 Mix together the flour, turmeric, asafoetida (if using), fenugreek, chilli powder, coriander, cumin, ginger and 1 tablespoon of the oil, then add 100 ml (3½ fl oz) tepid water and knead the mixture for 5 minutes into a soft pliable dough. Leave the dough in a bowl covered in cling film for 10–15 minutes.

2 Divide the dough into 6 equal-sized balls. Use a clean damp tea towel to cover those not being worked with to stop the dough drying out. Take each ball and, with a dusting of flour, roll out into a 12.5 cm (5 inch) disc about 2 mm (¹⁄₁₀ inch) thick.

3 Heat a griddle and preheat a warm oven. When the griddle is hot, add 1 teaspoon of the oil and place a disc on to the griddle. Cook for about 1½ minutes on each side, carefully pressing the disc firmly down so that the whole surface is cooked. Cover with foil and place in the warm oven while you cook the remaining discs, adding 1 teaspoon of oil each time.

4 Serve hot with a mixed vegetable curry.

Indian Sweet Naan
Sheermal

MAKES 6

300 g (10 oz) plain flour, plus a little extra for dusting

2 teaspoons sugar

1 teaspoon rapid-action dried yeast

2 tablespoons plain yogurt

200 ml (7 fl oz) semi-skimmed or full-fat milk

a few saffron strands

Sheermal is a traditional saffron-flavoured unleavened bread similar to naan that is prepared with a dough consisting of plain flour, yeast and yogurt. Although the bread is sweet, it can be eaten with hot curries.

1 Put the flour into a large bowl and mix with the remaining ingredients.

2 Knead the resulting dough for 6 minutes, then cover with a clean damp tea towel and leave to rise for 1 hour.

3 Towards the end of that hour, preheat the oven to 200°C/400°F/gas mark 6.

4 Punch the dough and knead it again for a couple of minutes. Divide into 6 balls.

5 Lightly flour the work surface and roll each ball into a round shape about 5 mm (¼ inch) thick and 15 cm (6 inches) in diameter. Do not roll them out too thinly or they will be too crisp.

6 Carefully put the Sheermal on a baking tray or a sheet of foil and place in the centre of the oven. Bake for 10–12 minutes, until they puff up slightly and are golden and flaky. Serve hot.

Pea-stuffed Bread

Koraishutir Kochuri

MAKES 16

- 150 g (5 oz) frozen peas
- 2 green chillies, finely chopped
- ¼ teaspoon ground cinnamon
- ½ teaspoon salt
- ½ teaspoon ground coriander
- 5 cm (2 inch) piece of fresh root ginger, peeled and grated
- 450 ml (¾ pint) sunflower oil
- 100 g (3½ oz) plain flour
- 100 g (3½ oz) wholemeal flour

Made with fresh green peas, these are savoury deep-fried breads that can simply be eaten with a chutney or a pickle.

1 Cook the peas, drain and leave to cool. When the peas have cooled down, using a pestle and mortar, mash the peas with the chilli, cinnamon, salt, coriander and ginger until it becomes a coarse paste.

2 Heat 2 teaspoons of the oil in a frying pan and tip in the pea paste. Cook for 2 minutes, stirring occasionally, then remove from the heat and allow to cool.

3 To make the flour dough, combine the plain and wholemeal flour in a bowl and add 3–4 tablespoons of water – just enough to make a stiff dough. Knead the dough for 10 minutes and incorporate the mashed pea mixture. Knead the dough for a further 2 minutes, blending the pea mixture evenly into the dough. Then cover with a clean damp cloth to prevent it from drying out.

4 Heat the remaining oil in a deep-fryer or wok to 180°C/350°F. Add a small piece of dough to the oil: when the dough sizzles and rises to the surface, the oil is hot enough.

5 Take a small piece of dough the size of a squash ball and roll it out on a lightly oiled surface into a 10 cm (4 inch) disc about 3 mm (⅛ inch) thick. Repeat with the rest of the dough and cover each with a clean damp tea towel.

6 Add 2 discs to the deep-fryer at a time and turn them over when they puff up – this usually takes about 30 seconds. Quickly remove them when they begin to turn light brown. Drain on kitchen paper, being careful not to squash out the air. Serve immediately with hot tea.

Puffed Unleavened Bread
Phulka

MAKES 5–6

200 g (7 oz) wholemeal flour, plus a little extra for dusting

1 teaspoon vegetable oil

butter or ghee, to serve

Phulkas are usually made and served around the time the meal is eaten. They are cooked fresh practically every day in almost every household in northern India. The Hindi term 'hulka phulka' means light and fluffy. They are also known as rotis or chapatis.

1 Sift the flour into a bowl and add the oil. Stir in enough tepid water to make a soft dough – about 125 ml (4 fl oz). Knead for 10 minutes. The dough should not be sticky. Break off golf-ball-sized pieces of dough and roll these out on a floured surface into circles about 15 cm (6 inches) in diameter. As you roll, dust the phulka with a little flour, to prevent it from sticking and allowing the rolling pin to move freely.

2 Heat a heavy-based frying pan over a medium heat. Place a circle of dough in the pan and cook for 20 seconds on one side, then turn it over and wait until bubbles rise to the surface. Turn it over again and allow the first side to cook. With the back of a tablespoon, press firmly around the edges so the phulka puffs up. Repeat with the remaining dough.

3 Serve immediately brushed with a little butter or ghee or leave just plain. Traditionally phulkas are eaten with Aloo Gobhi (see page 72), Laal Maas (see page 32) and Shahi Paneer (see page 74).

Savoury Steamed Gram Flour Cake
Dhokla

350 g (11½ oz) gram flour (besan)

250 g (8 oz) yogurt, whipped

1½ teaspoons salt

1 teaspoon peeled and grated fresh root ginger or ginger paste

2 green chillies, very finely chopped or minced

½ teaspoon turmeric powder

1 teaspoon bicarbonate of soda

1 teaspoon groundnut or sunflower oil, plus extra for greasing

1 teaspoon lemon juice

TO SERVE

2 teaspoons groundnut or sunflower oil

1 teaspoon brown or black mustard seeds

a few curry leaves

a few coriander leaves, chopped

2–3 green chillies, slit lengthways

Dhoklas are steamed savoury snacks from Gujarat in western India. They are made from fermented gram flour or besan.

1 In a bowl, whisk the gram flour and yogurt together to make a smooth thick batter. You can add a little water if the batter is too thick. Mix in the salt and set aside for 4 hours covered with a lid.

2 Using a pestle and mortar, crush the ginger and green chillies together into a coarse paste. Add this to the batter together with the turmeric powder and mix well.

3 Mix the bicarbonate of soda, oil and lemon juice in a small bowl. Add this to the batter and combine well.

4 Take a square baking dish (10 x 10 x 5 cm/ 4 x 4 x 2 inches) that will fit into a steamer or a pressure cooker, and grease with a little oil. Pour the batter into the greased dish and steam for 15–20 minutes or until firm and spongy.

5 Allow to cool. Carefully remove the cooked batter from the pan and cut into 5 cm (2 inch) cubes. Place on a serving plate.

6 To serve, heat the oil in a small pan and add the mustard seeds and curry leaves, and heat until the seeds splutter. Remove from the heat and pour the mixture over the dhokla.

7 Garnish the with the coriander and green chillies. They can be served hot or cold with coconut chutney.

Bengali Samosa
Shingara

MAKES 12
SAMOSAS

300 g (10 oz) wholemeal flour, plus more for dusting

½ teaspoon baking powder

1½ teaspoons salt

vegetable oil, for deep-frying

½ teaspoon panch phoran (see page 54)

½ teaspoon turmeric

1 teaspoon peeled and grated fresh root ginger

pinch of asafoetida

4 green finger chillies, finely chopped

500 g (1 lb) white or red potatoes, peeled, boiled until tender, then lightly crushed

This is the Bengali version of the celebrated samosa from the north of India – a small triangular pastry filled with spiced vegetables and deep-fried. A tamarind chutney can be served with this at teatime.

1 Sieve the flour into a bowl with the baking powder and ¼ teaspoon of the salt. Stir in 150 ml (¼ pint) cold water, then knead for 5 minutes until it forms a smooth dough. Place in a clean bowl, cover with a plate and set aside for 30 minutes.

2 Heat 2 tablespoons of oil in a wok and add the panch phoran. Once the seeds splutter, add the turmeric, ginger, remaining salt and the asafoetida. Stir, then add the chillies, followed by the crushed potatoes. Sauté for 2 minutes.

3 Heat a frying pan or a griddle over a gentle heat. In a small bowl, mix a little flour with a few drops of water to make a thick glue. Divide the dough into 12 equal balls. Roll out each ball of dough to a 12 cm (5 inch) circle, flouring your surface to prevent it from sticking.

4 Place the circles on the griddle for 30 seconds each, then remove – this makes them easier to handle. Cut each circle in half. Take one semicircle, apply a little of the flour glue to half the straight edge, then fold into a cone shape overlapping by 5 mm (¼ inch) and press to seal.

5 Hold the cone with the pointed end downwards and fill with 1 tablespoon of the potato mixture. Seal the shingara with more flour glue, pressing the edges firmly together.

6 Heat the oil for deep-frying to 180°C/350°F. Fry the shingaras in batches for 3–4 minutes until golden brown. Remove with a slotted spoon and drain on kitchen paper. Serve hot.

Fenugreek Leaves with Potatoes
Methi Aloo

SERVES 4

400 g (13 oz) potatoes, peeled and chopped into 2.5 cm (1 inch) pieces

2 tablespoons sunflower or vegetable oil

1–2 garlic cloves, chopped

½ teaspoon chilli powder

½ teaspoon ground cumin

½ teaspoon salt

1 teaspoon tomato purée

3 tablespoons dried fenugreek leaves

Both the leaves and the seeds of the fenugreek plant are used extensively in Indian cooking. This is a dish using dried fenugreek leaves and is combined with potatoes, which assist in taking away the bitter edge to this herb.

1 Place the potatoes in a saucepan and top with just-boiled water. Boil for 8 minutes. Drain and set aside.

2 Heat a frying pan and add the oil. Tip in the garlic and the potatoes, and fry for 3–4 minutes until the potatoes have brown edges.

3 Add the chilli powder, cumin and salt, and mix. Stir in the tomato purée. Add the fenugreek leaves and cook for a further 2 minutes. Serve hot with Phulkas (see page 106).

Spiced Bengal Gram
Chholar Dal

SERVES 4

150 g (5 oz) bengal gram

¼ teaspoon turmeric

1 green finger chilli, slit lengthways

2 tablespoons mustard oil or groundnut oil

1 bay leaf

pinch of asafoetida

2 green cardamoms, slightly crushed

2.5 cm (1 inch) cinnamon stick

¼ teaspoon nigella seeds

2 medium dried red chillies, stalks removed

1 teaspoon ground cumin

2 tablespoons coconut cream, plus extra to serve

¼ teaspoon salt

Bengal gram is also known as chana dal or gram lentils. It is the most widely grown lentil in India. Matt yellow, with a rich nutty taste, gram lentils are used for making this dal, which is often served after a Hindu prayer ceremony.

1 Pick over the lentils to check for stones, then place in a sieve and wash under cold running water. Soak the lentils for 2 hours in 400 ml (14 fl oz) cold water.

2 Drain the lentils and place in a saucepan with 250 ml (8 fl oz) boiling water, the turmeric and green chilli. Simmer gently for 15–20 minutes or until the lentils are tender. Discard the green chilli and purée half the lentils in a blender. Set aside.

3 Heat the oil in a heavy-based pan. Add the bay leaf, asafoetida, cardamoms, cinnamon, nigella seeds, red chillies and cumin. Stir for a minute and then carefully add the coconut cream and salt. Mix well. Tip in all the lentils, stir and simmer for 5 minutes.

4 Garnish with a swirl of coconut cream and serve hot with Basmati Chawal (see page 124).

Parsi Potatoes
Khara Papeta

SERVES 4

2 tablespoons sunflower
  or groundnut oil

1 teaspoon cumin seeds

1 medium onion, sliced

2 garlic cloves, crushed

1 green chilli, chopped

5 cm (2 inch) piece of
  fresh root ginger,
  peeled and grated

¼ teaspoon salt

400 g (13 oz) potatoes,
  peeled and cut into
    2.5 cm (1 inch) cubes

  a few coriander
    leaves for
    garnish,
    chopped

Parsis, who emigrated from Iran more than 1,000 years ago, have influenced the food in Mumbai and their rich spicy cuisine draws influences from a variety of international cooking techniques.

1 Heat a heavy-based pan and add the oil. After a minute, tip in a few of the cumin seeds. If they start to sizzle, the oil is hot enough. Add the remaining seeds to the oil. Stir for a minute, then tip in the onion. Fry for 4 minutes until the onion is translucent.

2 Stir in the garlic, chilli, ginger and salt. Tip the potatoes into the pan and mix well. Cover the pan and leave the mixture to simmer for 9–10 minutes until the potatoes are tender. Garnish with coriander leaves and serve hot.

Battered Potato Balls
Batata Vada

MAKES 10-12

vegetable oil, for deep-frying

½ teaspoon brown mustard seeds

½ teaspoon turmeric

¾ teaspoon salt

1 teaspoon granulated sugar

2 green finger chillies, finely chopped

625 g (1¼ lb) white or red potatoes, peeled, boiled and coarsely chopped

30 g (1 oz) coriander leaves, chopped

150 g (5 oz) gram flour (besan)

¼ teaspoon ground cumin

¼ teaspoon baking powder

These are a street food from Mumbai, sold around beaches and in fast-food restaurants. Batata vadas are the western Indian version of the north's samosas, but they are made with gram flour or besan rather than wheat flour.

1 Heat 1 tablespoon of the oil in a heavy-based pan large enough to hold the potatoes. When the oil is hot, gently tip in the mustard seeds, followed by the turmeric, ½ teaspoon of the salt, the sugar and chillies, and mix. Add the cooked potatoes, coarsely mashing as you mix. Add the coriander leaves and mash to make a lumpy mixture. Remove from the heat and leave to cool.

2 Sift the gram flour and remaining salt into a bowl. Add the cumin, baking powder, 1 teaspoon of the oil and 125 ml (4 fl oz) of cold water to make a batter the consistency of runny honey.

3 Wet your hands and roll the mash into pieces the size of golf balls.

4 Heat the oil in a deep-fryer or wok to 190°C/375°F. Drop a little batter into the oil: if it sizzles, the oil is hot enough. Dip the potato balls in the batter and coat them evenly. In batches, drop the coated balls into the hot oil and fry for 4 minutes, or until the outside of the balls are a deep golden brown. Lift them out with a slotted spoon and drain on kitchen paper. Wrap in foil and keep warm while cooking the remaining potato balls. Serve hot with Dhaniyein ki Chatni (see page 126).

Indian Cheese Bites
Paneer Tikka

SERVES 6

½ teaspoon garam
masala (see page 14)

1 tablespoon plain flour

½ teaspoon crushed
dried red chillies or
hot chilli powder

¼ teaspoon crushed
black peppercorns

2 teaspoons ground
cumin

2 tablespoons malt
vinegar

½ teaspoon salt

300 g (10 oz) paneer,
cut into 2.5 cm (1 inch)
cubes

1 medium onion, cut
into 2.5 cm (1 inch)
chunks

1 green pepper,
deseeded and cut into
2.5 cm (1 inch) chunks

2 tablespoons vegetable
oil

Indian cheese or paneer is a must in the vegetarian Punjabi menu. Paneer is made from whole cow's milk curdled with lemon juice and then pressed until its texture is firm and similar to tofu. Tikka means piece.

1 Mix together the garam masala, flour, chilli, pepper, cumin, vinegar and salt. Stir the paneer cubes into this marinade, cover and leave for at least 10 minutes in a refrigerator.

2 Soak 6 wooden skewers in water for 15 minutes. Preheat the oven to 180°C/350°F/gas mark 4 or preheat the grill to medium.

3 Thread the paneer on to the skewers, alternating the cheese with chunks of onion and green pepper. Brush with vegetable oil, then roast or grill for 10 minutes, turning occasionally, until the paneer is golden yellow.

4 Serve hot with onion salad and Dhaniyein ki Chatni (see page 126).

Chilli Indian Cheese

Mirch Waala Paneer

SERVES 2−3

1 teaspoon cornflour

pinch of salt

1 teaspoon plain flour

225 g (7½ oz) paneer, cut into 2.5 cm (1 inch) cubes

3 tablespoons vegetable oil

2 green finger chillies

1 garlic clove, crushed

1 teaspoon white or demerara sugar

¼ teaspoon ground black pepper

1 tablespoon malt vinegar

1 tablespoon tomato ketchup

1 tablespoon dark soy sauce

1 tablespoon hot chilli sauce

1 medium onion, thinly sliced into rings

Paneer is used throughout India in a variety of dishes, especially in the north. It's an essential source of protein in many vegetarian diets and chilli paneer is the vegetarian version of chilli chicken or barbecued spare ribs.

1 Mix together the cornflour, salt and flour with 1 tablespoon of cold water to make a thin paste. Coat the paneer in the paste.

2 Heat the oil in a frying pan and lightly fry the paneer cubes for 5 minutes until golden. Remove with a slotted spoon, drain on kitchen paper and set aside.

3 In the same pan over a low heat, gently fry the whole green chillies, garlic, sugar, black pepper, vinegar, tomato ketchup, soy sauce and chilli sauce with 2 tablespoons boiling water for a couple of minutes. Add the paneer and mix well, smothering the paneer cubes with the sauce.

4 Serve hot in a Phulka (see page 106) with onion rings.

Rice with Cumin Seeds
Jeera Chawal

SERVES 6

300 g (10 oz) white basmati rice

1 tablespoon vegetable oil

1 teaspoon cumin seeds

¼ teaspoon salt

15 g (½ oz) butter or ghee

The Punjabis in northern India are predominantly a wheat-eating people, but they cook 'seasoned' rice on special occasions. Plain or steamed rice is only eaten when someone is feeling under the weather.

1 Rinse the rice thoroughly under cold running water.

2 Heat the oil in a heavy-based saucepan. Add the cumin seeds and stir for a few seconds, allowing them to sizzle but not burn. Add the rice and salt. Stir so the oil coats all the rice and it looks glossy.

3 Pour in 600 ml (1 pint) boiling water and add the butter or ghee. Cover and simmer without stirring on a low heat for 10 minutes or until the grains are tender (all the water should be absorbed by the rice).

4 Serve hot with Dal Makhani (see page 125).

Lemon Rice
Elemicha Sadam

SERVES 2−3

200 g (7 oz) white basmati rice

1 teaspoon skinned split black lentils or urad dal

1 tablespoon groundnut or vegetable oil

½ teaspoon brown or black mustard seeds

2 medium dried red chillies

5–6 curry leaves

¼ teaspoon salt

¼ teaspoon turmeric

1 tablespoon lemon juice

Before cooking basmati rice, rinse the grains thoroughly in cold running water to remove any starchy residue: this makes it less sticky when cooked.

1 Rinse the rice in a colander or sieve under cold running water for at least 30 seconds. Pick over the lentils to check for small stones.

2 Heat the oil in a heavy-based saucepan. Add the mustard seeds. When they pop and crackle, add the lentils, red chillies, curry leaves, salt and turmeric, and stir for a few seconds.

3 Add the rice and mix well, then pour in 500 ml (17 fl oz) boiling water. Cover tightly and simmer over a low heat for 5 minutes. Add the lemon juice. Replace the lid and simmer for a further 8 minutes (all the water should be absorbed by the rice).

4 Serve hot with Kerala Kozhi Eshstu (see page 26).

Plain Basmati Rice
Basmati Chawal

SERVES 2–3

200 g (7 oz) white basmati rice

¼ teaspoon salt (optional)

drop of vegetable oil

Basmati is a small but long grain aromatic rice with a nut-like flavour and aroma. Originating from south-east Asia, it is the most expensive rice in the world.

1 Rinse the rice in a colander or sieve under cold running water for at least 30 seconds. Place in a saucepan with the salt (if using) and the oil, and stir. Add 375 ml (13 fl oz) boiling water and cover the pan. Simmer on a very low heat for 10 minutes.

2 Remove the lid and, with a fork, check a few of the grains to see if they're cooked – all the water should be absorbed by the rice.

3 Cooled, cooked rice can be stored in the refrigerator for 24 hours only. When reheating rice, warm it in a pan on a very low heat with 1 teaspoon of butter, ghee or oil. Make sure it is piping hot before serving.

Buttered Spiced Black Lentils
Dal Makhani

125 g (4 oz) whole black lentils or whole urad dal

75 g (3 oz) butter or ghee

pinch of asafoetida (optional)

1 medium onion, finely chopped

2 green finger chillies, finely chopped

2 garlic cloves, finely chopped

¼ teaspoon salt

½ teaspoon turmeric

¼ teaspoon hot chilli powder

1 teaspoon ground coriander

1 teaspoon ground cumin

125 g (4 oz) cooked kidney beans

1 teaspoon peeled and finely grated fresh root ginger

¼ teaspoon garam masala (see page 14)

2 tablespoons single cream

handful of coriander leaves, chopped

In rural Punjab, al fresco eating mainly occurs in self-service, roadside food joints called dhabas, frequented by truck drivers and travellers. They always serve Dal Makhani, which is cooked on a slow fire, often simmering for hours until the lentils turn creamy.

1 Check through the black lentils for small stones, place in a sieve and rinse under cold running water. Soak the lentils in 300 ml (½ pint) cold water for 8 hours or overnight.

2 Rinse the lentils, then place in a saucepan with 400 ml (14 fl oz) boiling water. Bring to the boil. Cover and simmer for 30 minutes, until the lentils are tender.

3 In a pan, melt 50 g (2 oz) of the butter. Add the asafoetida (if using) and stir. Tip in the onion, chillies and garlic, and gently fry for 7 minutes or until golden, stirring occasionally.

4 Add the salt, turmeric, chilli powder, coriander and cumin, followed by the cooked kidney beans, lentils and their cooking water. Mix and add the ginger. Fry over a medium heat for 5 minutes, stirring occasionally. Add 400 ml (14 fl oz) boiling water and simmer for 10 minutes.

5 Sprinkle over the garam masala and put the remaining butter on top. Swirl in the cream and sprinkle over the coriander before serving.

Coriander Chutney
Dhaniyein ki Chatni

SERVES 6

100 g (3½ oz) coriander leaves, roughly chopped

3 green finger chillies, roughly chopped

1 garlic clove, roughly chopped (optional)

½ teaspoon salt

1 teaspoon lemon juice

1 teaspoon demerara sugar

Coriander chutney is an eternal favourite: it goes well with many snacks, such as pakoras or moong dal chilas.

1 Place all the ingredients in a blender and blitz until the mixture becomes a coarse paste: add 4–5 tablespoons of cold water to ease blending. Alternatively, use a pestle and mortar.

2 This chutney can be stored in an airtight, non-metallic container for up to 4 days in the refrigerator.

Mint Chutney
Pudinay ki Chatni

SERVES 4

50 g (2 oz) mint leaves

1 medium onion,
roughly chopped

2 green finger chillies,
roughly chopped

1 tablespoon lemon
juice

½ teaspoon salt

25 g (1 oz) coriander
leaves, roughly
chopped

1 teaspoon demerara
sugar

*Pudina ki Chatni is often prepared on the day it is being served –
it will not keep overnight since the flavour starts to deteriorate
even when in the refrigerator.*

1 Place all the ingredients in a blender together with
3–4 tablespoons of water and blend well to form a
thick paste.

2 Serve immediately. This should be consumed the same
day as when made.

Quick Mango Pickle
Aam ka Achaar

MAKES 20
SERVINGS

625 g (1¼ lb) raw green mangoes, peeled and stoned

4 tablespoons vegetable oil

1 teaspoon brown or black mustard seeds

½ teaspoon turmeric

2 teaspoons hot chilli powder

½ teaspoon salt

4 teaspoons demerara sugar

Before convenience foods became the norm, Indian women were recognized for their expertise in preparing pickles – the most popular kind of preserve. There are literally hundreds of pickle recipes and no Indian meal is complete without one.

1 Cut the mango flesh into 1 cm (½ inch) cubes.

2 Heat the oil in a saucepan and tip in the mustard seeds. When they begin to splutter, add the turmeric followed by the mangoes, chilli powder, salt and sugar. Stir over a low heat for 4 minutes. Leave to cool.

3 Store in an airtight non-metallic container in the refrigerator for up to a week. Use as a relish alongside a main meal of mild dishes.

Seasoned Yogurt
Tadka Raita

SERVES 2−3

250 ml (8 fl oz) natural unsweetened yogurt

1 small onion, finely sliced

1 medium tomato, finely chopped

1 green finger chilli, finely chopped

¼ teaspoon salt

1 tablespoon vegetable oil

¼ teaspoon brown or black mustard seeds

4 curry leaves

10 unsalted peanuts (optional), skinned

Yogurt, or curd as it is known in India, is a staple throughout the regions. It is eaten plain or in raitas or hot chutneys with vegetables and fruit added. This cool yogurt salad is the perfect antidote to hot spicy dishes.

1 In a bowl, whip the yogurt until it is creamy. Fold in the onion, tomato, green chilli and salt.

2 Heat the oil in a small frying pan, then add the mustard seeds and curry leaves. Fry for a few seconds, then add the peanuts (if using). Fry for a minute, making sure they do not burn. Leave to cool.

3 When the mixture has cooled, gently add it to the yogurt. Serve chilled.

Sweet Lemon Pickle

Nimbu ka Achaar

SERVES 20

12 unwaxed medium
  lemons

150 g (5 oz) salt

300 g (10 oz) granulated
  sugar

1 teaspoon garam
  masala (see page 14)

1 tablespoon ajowan
  seeds

Lemon or lime pickle is ubiquitous throughout India. Pickles are mainly made during the summer months with vegetables and fruits such as mango, lime and green chillies. There are innumerable recipes for this pickle but my mother Kami's method is one of the simplest and contains only one spice and no oil.

1 Wash the lemons and soak in cold water for 30 minutes.

2 Dry the lemons, then top and tail them. Cut each one into 8 pieces by cutting them in half and then each half into 4 pieces. Mix the lemon pieces with all the other ingredients in a bowl.

3 Pour into a sterilized non-metallic airtight jar and keep in a warm place, like a cupboard, for a week. Every so often shake the jar to make sure the liquid covers all the pieces. When the lemons begin to turn dark, the pickle is ready to eat. It can be stored for up to 8 months.

4 Serve as a relish with any Indian dish, such as Parathas (see page 43) or Phulkas (see page 106) with Aloo Gobhi (see page 72).

Desserts

Apricot Nut Dessert
Malai Khumani

SERVES 4

50 g (2 oz) caster sugar

250 g (8 oz) dried apricots, roughly chopped

2 drops of rose water or vanilla essence

200 ml (7 fl oz) double cream, stiffly whipped

50 g (2 oz) chopped pistachios

Malai Khumani is a popular recipe that was created in the princely southern state of Hyderabad. This dessert is a favourite at weddings.

1 In a heavy-based pan, gently dissolve the sugar in 400 ml (14 fl oz) cold water, stirring occasionally until all the sugar has dissolved. Add 200 g (7 oz) of the dried apricots and simmer for 12 minutes. Drain.

2 Stir the rose water or vanilla essence into the whipped cream. Fold the apricots into the cream and spoon into 4 ramekins or serving glasses.

3 Serve chilled, garnished with the chopped pistachios and the remaining dried apricots.

Indian Spiced Yogurt Dessert
Shrikhand

SERVES 4

500 g (1 lb) Greek-style yogurt

2½ tablespoons caster sugar

10–12 saffron strands

a generous pinch of freshly grated nutmeg

This dessert comes from Maharashtra and is best prepared using full-fat yogurt or Greek-style yogurt to achieve a thick consistency. It is a dish that is now sold commercially in India but homemade is much better and more satisfying.

1 Place the yogurt on a large fine-mesh nylon sieve or in a large piece of muslin cloth. Put the sieve or cloth with the yogurt over a bowl, cover and refrigerate for at least 8 hours, or overnight to allow the whey to drain away.

2 Add the sugar, saffron and nutmeg to the strained yogurt and mix well.

3 Serve chilled.

140

DESSERTS

Indian Fudge
Doodh ki Barfi

SERVES 4

1 teaspoon unsalted
   butter

50 g (2 oz) caster sugar

150 ml (¼ pint) double
   cream

125 g (4 oz) full-fat milk
   powder

Milk barfi is the simplest of sweetmeats that can be flavoured with a hint of ground cardamom seeds or a few saffron strands for a little added spice if desired.

1 Melt the butter in a heavy-based saucepan, then add the sugar and stir continuously over a medium heat for 3 minutes. Add the cream and simmer for 3 minutes, then add the milk powder. Continue stirring for 5 minutes or until the mixture becomes stiff and thick and it begins to leave the sides of the pan.

2 Carefully place on to greaseproof paper and shape into a 10 cm (4 inch) square about 1.5 cm (¾ inch) thick. Leave to cool, then cut into 2.5 cm (1 inch) squares and serve. These can be stored in an airtight container in the refrigerator for a week. Remove from the refrigerator 10 minutes before serving.

Indian Fudge with Pistachios
Pista Barfi

SERVES 4

50 g (2 oz) unsalted
shelled pistachios

1 teaspoon unsalted
butter

50 g (2 oz) caster sugar

150 ml (¼ pint) double
cream

125 g (4 oz) full-fat milk
powder

3 tablespoons caster
sugar

½ teaspoon cardamom
seeds, crushed
(the seeds from
approximately
4–5 cardamoms)

Barfi is an Indian sweet made from milk that has been cooked slowly and reduced to a fudge-like consistency. It is then flavoured with select spices and other ingredients such as fruit and nuts. This is flavoured with pistachios and cut into bite-sized pieces.

1 Heat a frying pan over a medium heat, add the pistachios and gently toss for 2 minutes. Allow the pistachios to cool and then crush them using a pestle and mortar until they are coarsely ground.

2 Melt the butter in a heavy-based saucepan, then add the sugar and stir continuously over a medium heat for 3 minutes. Add the cream and simmer for 3 minutes, then add the milk powder. Continue stirring for another 3 minutes to combine the milk powder, then tip in the cardamom seeds and pistachios. Stir for 2 minutes or until the mixture becomes stiff and thick and it begins to leave the sides of the pan.

3 Turn the mixture out on a sheet of greaseproof paper and shape into a 10 cm (4 inch) square about 3.5 cm (1½ inch) thick.

4 Cover and cool in the refrigerator for 3 hours, then cut into 2.5 cm (1 inch) squares or diamonds. These can be stored in an airtight container in the refrigerator for a week. Remove from the refrigerator 10 minutes before serving.

Ground Rice Pudding
Phirni

SERVES 4

1 tablespoon unsalted almonds, cut into slivers

1 tablespoon unsalted pistachios, roughly chopped

750 ml (1¼ pints) full-fat milk

5 tablespoons rice flour

5 tablespoons caster sugar

1 teaspoon rose water (optional)

5 green cardamoms, seeds only, crushed

a few saffron strands (optional)

Phirni is a smooth and creamy Punjabi dessert. It is a chilled rice flour pudding laced with cardamom, and during the festival of Diwali rose water and saffron are often added.

1 Mix the almonds and pistachios together in a small bowl.

2 Gently heat the milk in a heavy-based pan. When it begins to boil, add the rice flour and sugar, and mix well. Cook over a low heat, stirring frequently, for 2 minutes to dissolve all the sugar.

3 Add half the chopped nuts to the milk with the rose water (if using). Continue cooking and occasionally stirring until the mixture thickens, like the consistency of thick custard.

4 Spoon into 4 small ramekins or serving cups, sprinkle over the remaining nuts and leave to cool. Refrigerate for at least 1 hour. Serve chilled, garnished with the cardamom seeds and saffron strands (if using).

Chilli Hot Chocolate
Masala Doodh

SERVES 2

50 g (2 oz) **dark chocolate 70% cocoa solids, plus extra to serve**

50 ml (2 fl oz) **single cream**

50 ml (2 fl oz) **full-fat milk**

50 g (2 oz) **drinking chocolate powder**

¼ teaspoon **ground cinnamon**

30 g (1 oz) **demerara sugar**

1 **dried medium red chilli, stalk removed**

chilli flakes, to serve

Indians love to spice things up and that includes anything sweet. I discovered this drink on the coast of Mumbai, where there were plenty of eateries serving spicy milkshakes and chilli-flavoured ice cream.

1 Break the chocolate into small pieces and place in a small heavy-based pan with all the other ingredients. Simmer gently over a low heat for 5 minutes, whisking occasionally, until the chocolate has dissolved.

2 Strain the mixture through a nylon sieve and serve immediately in small espresso cups sprinkled with a few chilli flakes and grated chocolate.

Acknowledgements

Executive Editor: Eleanor Maxfield
Senior Editor: Sybella Stephens
Art Direction and Design: Tracy Killick
Design Concept: Smith & Gilmour
Photographer: Noel Murphy
Home Economist: Sue Henderson
Home Economist's Assistants: Mark O'Brien and Tanya Sadourian
Stylist: Wei Tang
Senior Production Controller: Amanda Mackie